A man without a vision for the future will always live in the past.

Reverend A.R. Bernard
CHRISTIAN CULTURAL CENTER NEW YORK

"*Pardoned* is a story of personal triumphs and the miraculous power God brings to bear when we choose His call over the call of man. This story is universal. I continue to feel blessed by the power of Pastor Lee's message-that life's struggles can prepare us for the triumphs. After reading this, I felt as if I could run a marathon!"

Pam Shipp, Ph.D.
CENTER FOR CREATIVE LEADERSHIP

"For all of us, life is filled with paradox and contradiction. Could God be there too? *Pardoned* is the extraordinary story of a man who found God to be present even in the darkest recesses of life. Here is a book which stretches our theology and offers us hope. I recommend it heartily."

Dr. Robert K. Johnston
PROFESSOR OF THEOLOGY AND CULTURE
FULLER THEOLOGICAL SEMINARY

"The autobiography of Promise Lee is what every social reformer hopes for. That, given a second chance, the fallen will return to society and make a contribution. Pastor Lee returned to society and his work as a community organizer brought national honor to his city and state."

Sy A. Lee
SY A. LEE INVESTIGATIONS, INC.

P9-DXJ-221

"Promise Lee's story of ghetto to grace reads like a suspense thriller. One marvels at the twists and turns he takes on the path to redemption. It is a book that celebrates the prevailing goodness of God in the midst of the seemingly insurmountable challenges of the world."

Joseph B. Leininger
PRESIDENT & CEO, RESOURCE LAND HOLDINGS

"In a time when people are looking for someone to "be real," *Pardoned* takes it there and then some. The redemptive power of God the Father is demonstrated in one man's life that can be truly compared to the conversion of Paul the Apostle. Promise Lee is a man you would not have wanted to encounter on the other side of the cross and the kind of man you can't wait to encounter on this side of it."

Bill Paige
FORMER NYPD DETECTIVE, METROPOLITAN DIVISION
SPECIAL ASSISTANT TO THE PRESIDENT, YOUNG LIFE

"*Pardoned* makes me question my views of American traditions, education, race relations, God's mercy and redeeming power, Satan's powerlessness, God's timing and plan for us. Thanks so much for allowing me to share in your story. It is a gift to those who have yet to read it."

Jordan Bridwell
MISSIONARY TO *HIS PEOPLE CHURCH*
BLOEMFORTEIN, SOUTH AFRICA

Pardoned

A Judicial Memoir

Promise Lee

Relevant World

thank you

To my parents Promise & Fannie
for never giving up on me.

To my pastor, mentor, spiritual father and friend,
The Reverend A.R. Bernard
for helping me to see life from
God's point of view.

To the brothers on the inside
who watched my back when I couldn't
watch it myself.

To all who have contributed to my life directly and
indirectly— I may not have welcomed your lessons
at the time, but I am grateful for them now. You
helped write this book.

And to my wife, Juanita,
whose dove-like spirit has helped me find
balance in this season of life.

Thank you.

FOREWORD

Most of us are all too familiar with the stereotypes of and statistics about young African American men. If the stereotypes are to be believed, African American males are less resourceful, less educated, more violent and more to be feared than any other demographic group. U.S. Justice Department statistics report that one in three black men age twenty-five and younger are either on probation, on parole or in prison. In fact, sadly, there are more young black men in jails and prisons than there are on college and university campuses.

There has been no lack of scholarship and discussion on this dismal reality.

Yet, there had been very little public discourse about how some are able to bounce back from such circumstances. About why they are different. About what makes survival possible for them.

That is the reason for this book.

In it, Pastor Promise Y. Lee tells his story--straight. No window dressing. No prettying it up. He tells it like it happened, and detail for sad and triumphant detail.

Still, it does not stop there. We also see, through his experiences, through his recollection of personal and world events, through his poetry and prose, how he was able to escape that life--and not only escape, but to make life better for others like him who come from the same community.

Did Promise Lee save himself? Did God save him? Was his salvation from the streets, a combination of self-will and divine intervention? Is there hope for others like him? How will that hope show itself?

These are the questions ultimately answered here.

But before you can get to the answers, you must lay out the territory from which they spring. And that is what is so compellingly and instructively laid out here: a snapshot of one life that can illuminate the lives of so many.

For those hungry for the answers to how African American men can be emancipated from their prisons, literal and figurative, *Pardoned* is the ultimate book of instruction.

Rosemary Harris
PRESIDENT, *COLORADO SPRINGS BRANCH OF THE NAACP*

table of contents

PARDONED

1: Earning My Number 15

2: The Common Denominator 19

3: In a Strange Land 23

4: On Being Black 25

5: Against Forgetting 32

6: Can't Live With 'Em, Can't Live Without 'Em 40

7: High and Bye 49

8: The Road to Hell 58

9: A Call vs. The Call 65

10: Full Alert 73

11: The Tide Turns and Turns Again .75

12: The First Night 79

13: Fish Tank 85

14: Diagnosis 89

15: Relieving the Pressure 94

16: I Chose the Dorm 97

17: M.S. 102

18: Testing Ground, Teaching Ground 108

19: Great Men 111

20: Buena Vista 116

21: I'm Back 122

22: You Never Can Go Home 129

23: Man Down 134

24: Never Look Back 137

25: On the Outside 145

26: Playing and Playing It Straight 150

27: Runnin' the World 158

28: In a Mirror, Dimly 162

29: Living Large 166

30: I Said Yes 169

31: Slowing and Sorting in the Silence 173

32: My New Life 177

33: Get a Job 181

34: Hillside 183

35: The Call 188

Afterword 191

a message to the reader

I went to prison at a very young age, years before my senior prom. I was fortunate. I survived. I have not been back, except to visit others.

The story you are about to read is fact, not fiction. It is a real account of my life from as far back as I can remember. I need to warn you, some of the writing is very graphic. I have toned down the language as much as possible without deviating from actuality. This story will raise many questions that unfortunately beg unfound answers. It will also offer answers to questions you may not have thought to ask.

Political theorist Hannah Arendt once said, "The sad truth is that most evil is done by people who never make up their mind to be good or evil." I didn't make up my mind until I was twenty-five. In fact, I hadn't even thought of the question. I was just living. Surviving in a way that made sense to me at the time. It is my hope that whichever side of the table you are on, you make up *your* mind.

Life has taught me how fragile the so-called human spirit is. It can be damaged or broken very easily. I have offended God because I have damaged the souls of his children, and it is the soul of mankind that God is most concerned about.

Over the years I have hurt many people, both intentionally and unintentionally. Each day I ask God to help me to do less harm.

My intent is not for this writing to be viewed as a way to profit over shed blood or offended souls, but to simply share from my limited experiences the power of redemption and warn against the agony of regret. As you read this book and experience life through my eyes, I encourage you to think about three things and do two: Think about the power of regret, the power of forgiveness, and the power of doing less harm. Then I encourage you to do the following: Respect and protect the souls of mankind.

PROMISE LEE
June, 2005

ONE

It was at about dusk on September 3, 1974, in Colorado Springs, when my friends, Larry White and Darrell White (not related), and I found ourselves incredibly bored. We decided to walk downtown to Acacia Park to hang out. The park was known for hippies and drug trafficking. You could get any kind of dope you wanted there.

The park was across the street from the YMCA and just down the street from the post office and New Joe's Club, where my friend Paul and I used to hang out a lot. But that had been a long time ago, and now Larry and Darrell and me were tight. We were Southsiders.

Now, Bijou Street ran along the south side of the park and we were there near the amphitheater when a van pulled up and a guy I hadn't seen before said, "Wanna buy some drugs?"

"What you got?" I asked.

"Some speed and some weed."

"Yeah, we want some. Wanna buy some acid?"

"Yeah, maybe we can make a trade."

We had a regular scam to get acid. First, Larry and I would borrow a car from one of our GI friends. We had to do this because we weren't old enough to have driver's licenses, let alone own a car.

Anyway, the scam was this: Larry would drive and I would sit in the passenger seat and we'd follow the milkman on his route. The milkman would put an order on the steps and we'd ride along behind him, then I'd jump out and pick up what he had just dropped off. We'd make his whole route and by the time it was over, we'd have an entire car full of milk and cottage cheese and stuff like that. Then we'd take it over to the hippies on the north side of town and trade it for acid. The hippies really loved that milk and stuff, so we always got paid.

These guys wanted to deal, so we jumped into the van with them and told them to drive toward the alley behind Larry's sister's house on Corona Street, about a mile away, so we could get the acid.

While we were driving over to the house, Hocking, the guy in the passenger seat, was passing the dope back to us so we could check it out. And the whole time Darrell was trying to steal both the weed and the speed. When we passed it back, the bags were short.

When we got ready to go inside, LaFurge, the driver said, "One of you has to stay here. Have him stay." He pointed to Darrell because they knew he had the missing stuff. That's when we knew that they knew.

So Larry and I ran into the house and while Larry got the acid, I went and got my piece. It was a big pistol, a .22 Magnum and it always reminded me of the one Matt Dillon had on *Gunsmoke*. I methodically loaded the gun with hollow point bullets and shoved it down my pants. Hollow points were more deadly because they exploded on impact. The whole time I was doing this, I guess I was thinking I was going to rob them. I don't know what I was thinking... if I was going to rob them, or if I knew there was bound to be some funny stuff because of Darrell, or what. Anyway, we headed back out to the van with the acid and the gun.

As we approached, there was a struggle going on. LaFurge and Hocking both had slammed Darrell up against the far side of the van between a retaining wall in the alley. It had grown pretty dark, so it was hard to see exactly what was going on, but I knew Darrell was in trouble.

I called out, "Let him go."

Hocking, who had seen Darrell trying to steal their stuff, called back, "This MF is trying to rip us off!"

I said again, "Let him go."

"You goddamned MFs are trying to rip us off!"

"I won't tell you again, let him go."

So Hocking let go of Darrell and started to come around to the front of the van where I was standing. At the same time, Darrell turned around and grabbed LaFurge. Larry jumped into the van to get the stuff.

Hocking never stopped. He just kept coming toward me, pulling out some nunchucks and swinging them. He was a huge guy, six foot two and over two hundred pounds. I was five foot six and one forty-five.

I said, "Look, don't come any further."

But he kept on coming. I guess he thought I was bluffing. And it was dark, so he couldn't see the handle of the gun sticking out of my pants.

I told him again, "Just stop where you are."

He just kept coming and swinging those nunchucks so I said, "You're going to make me shoot you." Then I pulled the gun out.

"Stop!" I shouted.

But Hocking didn't stop. So I shot him in the stomach. He collapsed without a sound.

"Put him in the van," I ordered LaFurge. But his friend was pretty stunned and didn't move.

"Put him in the van I said." By this time Larry was out of the van and had all the weed and the speed and the money. Finally, LaFurge dragged Hocking into the van and took off for the hospital.

Larry and Darrell and I went into the house and split up the stuff. I didn't feel anything. I didn't feel scared. I didn't feel sad. I didn't feel happy. I didn't feel anything. *I had stopped feeling a long time ago.* The fact that death was a part of life was clear to me. It was as mundane as eating cornflakes in the morning.

Daniel Hocking died seventeen days later on September 20, 1974, at the age of twenty. I heard about it while in the county jail, charged with armed robbery and assault. That day, the charges were changed to MURDER in the first degree.

It all began with me playing in our front yard on Hancock Street in Colorado Springs. We had a bush with yellow flowers and in the springtime it would be surrounded by bees. I'd walk close to it and hit the bush to see the bees fly away, only to return some time later. I used to catch them in my hand and shake them up. Then, when I would open my hand, they would fly out.

One day I caught one and shook him up and opened my hand and he just laid there, and then finally stung me. The pain was excruciating. I ran into the house screaming. Mom looked at my hand. She nursed it and explained that because the bee lost his stinger in me, he would soon die. I thought about that for a long time. Why did God or nature or anybody make something with a protective device to defend itself, but you died if you used it? That really puzzled me.

I learned early in life that you're here today, gone tomorrow. When I was a child, death was a constant acquaintance. Many people died around me while I was in my preteen and teen years:

Cha Cha, who jumped out of our car and was run over

David Jr., who drowned in Texas

Big Mama, who, at age sixty-nine, died of diabetes

Tony Maxwell, who drowned in Prospect Lake

Paul and Rodney Price, who were killed in a car wreck

Mickey Adams, who was shot by a policeman

Nochie, who died of sickle-cell anemia

Rickey Lewis, who was shot with a sawed-off shotgun

Umwilu, who was stabbed in the Pen

And Daniel Hocking, who was shot in the stomach... by me.

Two

Death was my constant companion. My cousin David Jr., who I never really knew, drowned in Texas while swimming with some other boys in a water hole. He was thirteen years old. We went to the funeral. My dad was really serious, and still is, about family supporting family, whether through crisis or investments. Anyway, I found myself dressed up in a suit and under what seemed to be a large revival tent. My father told me to go up and look in the casket. So I did. I walked straight up to it, looked at the dead body for a while and came back to my seat. Later I heard a discussion between relatives and my dad. They didn't think I should have been made to look at the body because of my age. It really didn't affect me.

The way they reacted, everyone else seemed to be blaming God: crying, sad, in shock—and yet these were religious people. Those whom I always really felt knew the most about God. I remember the types of songs that were sung at David Jr.'s funeral. *Precious Lord* and *I'll Fly Away.* Songs that spoke about his flying away and going to a better place. A place where God was. Then I thought about the bee that had stung me in front of our house on Hancock Street. He didn't fly away, and if my cousin David Jr. was going to a better place, why was everyone so sad?

Well, after that, and even still today, sadness remains. They still talk about David Jr. not being here, as if God made a mistake.

During this period of my life, when I was around eight years old, I also became acquainted with the disabilities other people had. How different other people were. There were girls I knew, in fact, a whole family, that had very bad asthma. A boy who was humongously large (fat); a girl who had the shakes (which I later learned was called cerebral palsy); people who wore thick, thick glasses; a girl with polio who wore a big shoe; and of course my brother, Thurmas, who was, and is, deaf. *Why were things like this, God? Why was every-one so different? Why did some have more than others?* I didn't understand, but it seemed that these people were humble, and even then, I felt that I was there to make sure they didn't lose their stingers.

Well, another death, my grandmother on Daddy's side, hap-pened in the summer of 1972. But right before she died, I recall my mother driving us to school with our dog, Cha Cha, a Chinese pug. When we got close to the school, Cha Cha jumped out of the car and ran. It seemed like slow motion as we watched a blue car approach her. BOOM! Rumble, Rumble, SCREECH. She was hit. We jumped out. She was laying there on the street, bleeding from the mouth with her tongue hanging out. The car had literally knocked the crap out of her. I was going to save this life but the adults took over. Mom told us to go ahead to school and she'd take care of things. They assured me that after taking the dog to the vet, she'd be okay. Somehow I knew that wasn't true. If only I could work on her. If I could just hold her for a minute, she'd be okay. All day at school I wondered. *Around 10:00 a.m. I felt her die.* We were supposed to catch the bus home that day, but Mom picked us up. When we got in the car I said, "The dog died, didn't she?"

Mom answered, "Yes."

The ride home was very quiet and very long.

As I said, the summer of 1972 stays in my mind because of the death of my grandmother. She had been sick and I couldn't see how this could be. She was strong and healthy and good to people and at the same time seemed to be too mean to die.

My dad had dreamed about bananas and blood the night before she died, and his dreams had always been somewhat prophetic. My parents headed for Texas and I had to stay at the house of a white man named Gary Bohall. He used to pick us up for church and Sunday school when we were going to the "all white" church. His wife was kind and caring. And she could make some sandwiches. At home, we just had meat and bread. Mrs. Bohall added tomatoes and banana peppers. I never imagined things like these and still like my sandwiches that way today. We stayed with them for about a week and man, it was boring! We watched the Olympics on TV and ate sandwiches the whole time. But, Gary was a man who cared. He seemed to be a real Christian. Yes, this was a man who cared.

I remember the sadness of my father when they returned from Texas. He had lost his mother to diabetes and the sadness really seemed to linger on. As for my mother, she didn't seem to be affected much. Later, when she lost her dad, Whitehead, she seemed to take it quite well, wanting no sympathy, but simply support from her immediate family.

In 1968, when I was ten, my friend Tony Maxwell, who was twelve, was fishing at Prospect Lake in front of our house in Colorado Springs and jumped in the water off the dock. He never came back up. They came out and began dragging the lake, but he never surfaced. When they finally found him, he was swollen like a fat man. He had been about my size, but now he was swollen beyond looking real. He didn't have a neck and you couldn't see the break between his wrist and hand. If you stuck a pin in him, he looked like he'd explode. His father's face turned into a frown and it's still like that today. My, my, my, what the death of a loved one will do to people. When I see Mr. Maxwell now, I am always reminded of Tony because of the expression on his father's face.

I wonder why I didn't think of this later on when I caused other deaths. How many permanent frowns did I bring into the world?

That same year, Martin Luther King, Jr. was killed on April 4, just four days before my tenth birthday. I don't remember when I heard it first... on TV, radio or word of mouth, or even in the air. There was a quiet, all across the city, or at least in my neighborhood. Black people were silent. White people were quiet. Everyone seemed to be emotionally confused and frozen. Another death, this time from a distance, but seeming so close. Here it was, a man making a peaceful attempt at bringing peace for ALL people, and being gunned down. Live by the sword, die by the sword. Somehow that seemed to be a contradiction. And so, not only did my lessons on death continue, but also my lessons of life. King, a role model for Americans, black and white, gunned down. He didn't live by the gun but he died by it.

THREE

I watched the second hand surge forward on the face of our Big Ben alarm clock, but time never passed. The hands were eternally fixed at 2:00 a.m. and the fighting went on and on.

Thurmas, my youngest brother, slept undisturbed. His deafness shielded him from the truth. But Charmas, Thomas and I lay still in our beds, all blinking into the night and avoiding each other's eyes. At nine, ten, and twelve, we were already seasoned. We did not see, we did not feel, we did not talk. We only knew what another wave of shouts and insults forced us to know.

The rise and fall of angry voices again shredded the night and filled our minds with imaginings of what must be taking place, beyond our view. I could picture my mother with her long, black, beautiful hair draped softly across her shoulders, allowing the blood from her broken heart to pour, unchecked from her mouth. And my father's powerfully trim form, yearning for sophistication and education, but guilty of the adultery that had broken my mother's heart. This is what I saw in my mind, but from our beds we could see only the empty hallway and into the bathroom.

I longed for sleep and to be somewhere else. When I closed my eyes, I could hear the blood flowing in my veins and the rhythm of my heart. If I hadn't been bound by my position as the oldest to be on guard, I would have followed that rhythm right out of that house.

Footsteps raced down the hallway toward our room and pulled me back to reality. In the same instant my mother flashed past, the bathroom door slammed and the lock clicked. In nearly the same instant my father's body crashed against the locked door.

"COME OUT! COME OUT RIGHT NOW!" His fists pounded against the door. "DAMMIT, GET YOUR ASS OUT HERE!"

There was no escaping now. My father, full of rage, stood just feet from our open bedroom door. He pounded and shouted and shouted. I could imagine what I had become all too familiar with—the veins in his neck bulge and his nostrils flair.

Pain ripped through my body as the muscles in my leg knotted. I was rigid, ready to defend my mother.

In the next instant the shouting stopped. Then a gun blast ripped though our bathroom door.

Without knowing quite how I got there, I stood beside my father, looking inside the open door that seconds before had stood between my mother and danger. She was silent and slumped over, hit by the ricocheting bullet.

Now it was my turn to shout. I stood straight in my father's face, "YOU BETTER TAKE HER TO THE HOSPITAL. YOU BETTER TAKE HER TO THE HOSPITAL RIGHT NOW!"

"Move out the way, boy." He pushed me to the side, but I stayed on him to make sure he did the right thing. His face was blank now. All the rage had left. He looked old.

The next day I didn't go to school. I went to the hospital. I didn't go in, I just stood outside the hospital window—where I thought her room was—and looked in. Sonny Liston and Louis Armstrong died that year. And so did my faith in my father.

Then she came home. He brought her home. He was really taking care of her. Real, real nice. He was taking care of her as though it made up for everything. Maybe it did to her, but not to me. My anger was just beginning.

Four

It is a fortunate thing that every once in a while a person comes into our lives who forever changes us.

It was this way with my grandfather, Big Daddy Whitehead. Big Daddy taught me so much, not by what he said, but how he lived his life. And many would say that life had dealt him a cruel hand. It was in 1910 that his mother, my great-grandmother, Nancy, was working in Athens, Louisiana, as a maid for a wealthy white man named John A. Harris. At that time she had been married to a man named Buster for some years and they had several children. Like many recently emancipated families, they were still struggling to establish a living, own property, and earn a place in the society of the Deep South. It was in this context that Nancy was forced to bear an unfortunate, but common pain.

On a day in February of that year, she came to work seemingly prepared for what the day would bring. She busied herself with her regular duties, and eventually found herself alone with Mr. Harris. The rape that ensued resulted in the conception of my grandfather, Whitehead.

Despite the circumstances of her pregnancy, Buster put her out. Because of this, she needed her job now more than ever and so she continued to work for Mr. Harris.

After the baby was born, Nancy took him to work with her every day and Mr. Harris began to call him Whitehead because he had blond hair and blue eyes. He was able to "pass" and his name reflected that.

Over the next few years, Mr. Harris spent lots of time with Whitehead. And so one day, as Nancy and Whitehead were preparing to return home for the evening, Whitehead came right out and asked the old man why he and his mama couldn't just stay there.

Mr. Harris told him straight up, "Because you're colored. White folk and colored folk don't live in the same house together. Besides, my wife and real children wouldn't stand for you living here, even if you are my son."

So that settled where Whitehead would live, at least up until Nancy died of pneumonia. Whitehead was about four years old at that time and, out of necessity, he went to live with his mother's brother, Uncle George.

When Mr. Harris became gravely ill a short time later, he instructed Nancy's replacement, Mrs. Graham, to send for Uncle George and Whitehead. "But," he instructed her, "before you do, go out in the field and dig up the pot of money I've been saving for that boy." And then he explained just where she could find it.

Mrs. Graham did as she was told. She dug up the money and set it beside the old man's bed. Then she left in the wagon to get George and Whitehead. But before they could get back, Mr. Harris had died.

His sons confiscated the pot of money and threatened George and Whitehead with a horsewhip if they didn't get off the property immediately. The sons also refused to let Mrs. Graham drive them back. So George faced the long walk back with little Whitehead.

All that remained of Whitehead's inheritance was his name, and Whitehead continued to be his only name up until the time he went to school. Then, as was dictated by Louisiana law, he was forced to take first, middle and last names.

It was Whitehead himself who insisted on being called after the president, George Washington. And in order to satisfy the requirements for a middle name, a teacher wound up adding "General," making his full legal name General George Washington.

Despite being disowned by his father's family and despite the clear-cut separation between his father and him, Whitehead became a man of integrity. When he was grown, he worked at the Armory in town. Because of his physical appearance, he was granted promotional opportunities afforded only to whites in that day. He turned down each opportunity, one by one, in a symbolic gesture of solidarity with the other Black men—Black men who were overlooked strictly based on the color of their skin.

Yes, Whitehead was a great influence on my life, showing me in his actions what it means to be a proud black man. He never left the

Louisiana countryside, and in his hometown came to be known for his honesty and fairness. To me, he is one of the most successful men I have ever known. He raised a son and four daughters, one of them my mother. And he did it all without his due inheritance and without taking anything from the white man, except his name. When he died in 1993, at the age of eighty-three, hundreds of family, friends and acquaintances, including me, came to honor him.

My father also had a grandfather he admired—a blond, fair-skinned Dutchman who married my great-grandmother. He would sit in the back of the bus with his wife and when the bus driver would try to make him sit up front, he'd say, "I guess I know where I want to sit."

He would not be swayed from his convictions and he lived a life that was ahead of his time. Whether, in reality, he was a white Dutchman (as Daddy made him out) or a black man (as I saw him from the photo album), I could respect my great-granddad's conviction. It just wasn't as powerful as Whitehead's legacy and I quickly tired of my father's stories of him.

My father seemed to gravitate toward being white and that felt like betrayal to me. When his military career sent him to Canada and he took to learning French, and when he would try to make my brothers and sister and me learn to speak it too, it was more than I could bear. Whitehead had taught me what it was to be a black man, no matter what was on your family tree. He was proud to be a black man, even though he looked white. And here was Daddy, seemingly trying to do everything he could to put on the white man's ways. Didn't he know he was black?

My brother Charmas didn't. One of the few things I do remember from the early years is Charmas coming home one day, when he was about five or six, and asking what color he was. My mother asked, "What color do you think?"

"White?...Yellow?"

"Boy, don't you know you're black?"

Charmas didn't say anything more, but his face had this confused look. I knew what he was thinking, *My skin is light. How could*

I be black? But this was not something that even a big brother could explain. It was something he would have to learn on his own.

It's a funny thing. No matter who or what was on your family tree, and no matter what color your skin really is, there is always an abundance of folk wanting to convince you that you're a nigger—something inferior to the superiority in you.

One summer afternoon in 1967, when I was nine, Daddy and my brothers and I went to the store. As was usual in those days, we waited in the car while Daddy went in to make his purchases. It was a pretty new car, too. A Rambler station wagon. It felt good to ride in it. You could feel like a somebody in a big, new car. We had the windows open and my brothers and I were messing around, minding our own business. All of a sudden, the white kids in the car parked next to us started to talk real loud.

"Did you see all those bumps all over that man's face?" (My father had a number of moles.)

"I'd be embarrassed to have a dad that looked like that."

"It's okay, those are niggers. They don't care what their daddy looks like so long as they got one."

"Hey boy, is that nigger your dad?"

We tried to not pay attention, to ignore their insults, but our plan only brought down more wrath.

"Yep, that must be their daddy 'cause they're too dumb to answer. They're niggers, too."

"Look at that nose! See, I can make my nose like that." The ugly girl pressed her nose against the glass of the half-open window, pig fashion. She must have had a cold because it smeared all over the glass.

Right then Daddy came out. I wanted him to beat the tar out of them and their daddy, too. I was the oldest. I wanted to defend my honor and the honor of my family. I wanted to keep them from ever saying anything like that again to anybody. I wanted to be proud to be black and make them feel small and ashamed next to me.

Instead, all Daddy did was say, "Let it go. It doesn't matter. They're just ignorant."

This is still Daddy's philosophy. That people are just people and it shouldn't matter. He is probably right, it shouldn't matter. But it did, and those kids knew that.

Mom knew it too. She hated to be around white folks because they were so ignorant and rude. She felt this way because of how Whitehead was conceived and she felt this way because when Daddy was running around, he was running with white women.

My mom's thinking made more sense to me. With so many people around to tell me I was a nigger, I really had to consider if it was so. But in the end, I concluded that *if* I was a nigger, I was certainly a different kind of one.

I was in the third grade when a man came to school and brought a bearskin to show the class. I was really excited to see this thing, and while he was getting it out, he warned us not to rub our hands on the fur too hard. He said that if all the children were rough on it, the hair would fall out and then he wouldn't have a bearskin left to show other children.

While he was talking, I was so eager, I leaned way forward and stretched out my neck to see better. Finally he pulled it out and when I saw, I couldn't believe it. He had brought a polar bear skin!

I sat back, all my interest gone. I whispered to my friend sitting next to me, "Why did he bring a white bear? Why didn't he bring a black bear skin?"

How did he expect a white bear to have any meaning for me, when lines of black and white were so clearly drawn and it was clear I was black?

I beat up a kid at recess a little later that day. We were sent to the principal's office for fighting and he made us sweat. We sat on the bench for a long while. When he called us in, instead of really giving us some discipline, he said, "I'll tell you a secret if you promise to be good and not fight anymore, and if you promise not to tell anyone."

We told him, "Sure."

So he said, "There's going to be a fire drill today."

That was it! He sent us back to class. Sure enough, there was a fire drill that day, but I never understood the sense of what he did. He never asked us why we had the fight. And he never realized that he had sent a loud and clear message: I had full reign in his school. In fact, it was no longer his school. The authority now had to be shared.

After that, school never held much interest for me. We would read the same boring books over and over again. I never read about anyone who was like me, whether in the *Weekly Reader* or in our standard reading books. No one was like me. Not Dick, not Jane, not Sally. Not anyone in my class. Not anyone on the school faculty. Maybe the janitor or the cook.

I learned how big this gap was when I wrote out a definition of greens and was told that it was a color, not a food. And at lunch, I learned to notice that I didn't have a white bread sandwich precisely cut and neatly tucked into a sandwich bag, and I learned to be embarrassed when the grease from my leftover fried chicken soaked through the wax paper and my paper lunch sack.

What I would have really liked in school was a little science experiment, like mixing chemicals together or dissecting a frog. Things that I could learn by doing, not just reading. But we never had any of that.

So the fights continued and I rebelled against my teachers. I felt like I could whip them all. Just knock them out. I was feeling my physical oats.

A year later I was expelled from public schools, mainly for fighting. But in the end, it was because I urinated on a boy. He was using the stand-up toilet and I told him to get out of the way. He didn't move quick enough for me, so I peed on his back as he stood there, too scared to move. He finally got up the nerve and moved out of the way. I took my time and finished and went back to class. I was ten years old.

When I came into the classroom, I took a superball and bounced it up under the teacher's desk where her legs were. It was a closed-in desk with a vanity panel in the front, so when the ball got up under there it bounced a hundred times, and she was moving all around, trying to get away from it. Finally, she got up and she said, "That's it! Come on. I'm getting you out of here."

I was just waiting for her to put her hands on me because I really wanted to punch her, but she didn't. The principal even had a paddle, but he didn't use it. I wanted a confrontation. I was a man. I could prove it. I was no nigger. I could prove it. Instead, they expelled me.

I was sent to Sacred Heart Catholic School for the rest of the fifth. Being black is a state of mind, and it seemed that every day someone would tell us what that meant. Our young minds were shaped daily by not only angry screams of racial slurs and unfounded accusations, but also covert, subliminal rhetoric. We had an old-fashioned coat rack with a shelf and hooks and it was here that we put our coats and lunches. One day in the sixth grade, a girl's lunch turned up missing. The nuns said that they didn't know who took it, but that a black hand had been seen through the crack in the door grabbing the paper sack in question. Of course, to me and the other four non-white students in the school of more than two hundred, the message was clear: Even God must know that thieves were black if the nuns would say that. I did learn some things there at Sacred Heart, but this was the biggest and most damaging lesson of all.

Blackness is a state of mind.

FIVE

I don't really remember exactly how I met Paul Price, but, as far as I can recall, it was in 1971 at South Junior High. After about two years at Sacred Heart, the public schools decided to let me back in. So it was here that I met Paul. You talk about a hustler! Man, he was one.

I was drawn to him for a number of reasons. First, he looked like me. I was slightly taller and slightly darker, but otherwise, we were both lean and muscular, and we both had fairly bright colored skin the shade of carmel, and we both wore Afros as big as we could grow them. Because he was a little lighter than me, his hair was more sandy colored and mine was black. We both had black eyes. We wore the same size clothes and shoes. We even talked alike.

I guess it was because we were so much alike, and because we both had our scams, that a thing got started at school about how we should fight each other. They wanted to see who was going to be top dog. Or maybe they just wanted to see a good fight. I don't know.

Now normally, I would have quickly accepted the challenge and probably provoked him so that I could legitimately kick his butt. Back then in junior high, having a rep was very important. But when it came right down to it, I didn't really want to fight Paul and when I found out he didn't want to fight me either, we became friends. The best of friends.

We didn't have any classes together, so we could only hang out strong during lunch and before and after school. At the time, he lived on Vermijo Street just a few blocks away from me. Every morning we would meet in the alley behind my house so we could walk to school together. Even though we were both running the streets and feeling our oats, we went to school every day. There was action at school—girls, sports, friends. Paul was never late meeting me and so we were never late for school.

Along about Halloween time in the seventh grade, we started skipping classes so we could hang out downtown. South Junior High was just on the south end of the downtown area, so all we had to do was walk a couple of blocks and boom, we were in the heart of everything.

We would run lots of different scams when we were downtown. Sometimes we would hang out at the post office on the corner of Pikes Peak and Nevada Avenues and ask for money to buy stamps or even just panhandle.

Occasionally, we would meet Paul's older brother Rodney there and we would help him run the pigeon drop. When we did this, we were mostly just lending credibility to Rodney's scam. We were little kids. When he ran his con, Rodney would have an envelope full of toilet paper with a bill on top and bottom. He'd ask someone passing by if they'd hold the envelope for him. Of course, they always would because they'd think they were going to be the ones getting over. Somehow, though, Rodney would convince them to put their own money with his, to assure him they weren't going to scam him. Then Rodney would switch the envelopes and be gone. Usually, the passerby would split real quick too, thinking he had gotten the envelope with all the money. But Rodney was just too slick.

On other days we would go across the street to New Joe's, a nightclub that was open during the day. I could never figure out why it was called a nightclub. Lots of prostitutes would be there hustling all the soldiers, including colonels and generals. But lots of the military guys would be too nervous to set up their own dates. So, Paul and I would hang out there until someone would ask us to set up the deal. They would give us the money for the hooker, and then we would go out on the street and talk to the woman… about anything… the weather, other people, whatever. After a few minutes, we would go back in and tell the john that everything was set and that she was ready to go. He'd walk out to the woman and we'd get out of there as quick as we could, that is, before she could tell him we didn't give her any money and that she didn't do business like that anyway.

The officers were always so stupid. When they were trying to set up a deal, they would just pull their wallets right out and you could see just how much money they had.

This time, before anyone could say anything, Paul just reached over and snatched the wallet right out of the guy's hand.

Everybody just stood there for what seemed like a full minute. Everyone just looking at each other. The guy didn't jump up or anything. But I was scared to death. All of a sudden, Paul took off. Ran straight out the door. I jumped up and followed him, but he was already gone.

I was so scared, it seemed like I was running in slow motion and that I couldn't get out the door of the club and that my feet wouldn't move. And when I finally did get out the door, I looked up and down the sidewalk for Paul. All of a sudden, I saw him half way down the alley. He looked at me and smiled real big and waved his arm over his head and yelled, "Come on!"

I ran and only looked back once. I saw the guy standing by the door of the place. He saw me and I saw him. He kind of shrugged and nodded his head. He knew he'd been had and there was nothing he could do about it.

Even on the days we skipped classes, we always went back in the afternoon as school was letting out. For a while I had wood shop with Mr. Picket or gym or a few other classes that I would come back for. But even when I didn't have classes I enjoyed, I would come back for basketball or track practice. Paul would never play for the school team. I'm not sure why. But I did. So during that time he'd go home and then come back later to walk home with me.

It was always important to be there right when school was letting out. That's when all the fighting would go down and when you could get with your girl. There was a little store just a few blocks away and we'd take our girls in there and use the money we'd gotten to buy cokes and whatever they wanted. It was a real status thing to have bank.

My teachers would always be telling me to stop hanging around with the Prices. Otherwise, they warned, I was going to end up in the penitentiary.

One day I got called into the office by my counselor, Mrs.

Beatty. She was a very beautiful white woman, so I was quite happy to be in her office and just be looking at her. But I didn't get to day-dream for long. We wound up having a long talk that I must have listened to because I remember it to this day.

She said, "Promise, you're a bright young man. You're good looking. You have a good personality. You can go a long way in life. But you have to stop hanging around with the wrong crowd. Paul and Rodney are headed for Golden (the Boys Home)."

What she said just seemed like standard social worker talk. But at the time I tried to listen and I had a lot of questions. Like, I could never figure out what being good looking or any of that other stuff had to do with being successful. Who made up those rules? Who made those decisions?

I didn't ask her those questions, but after I left her office, I did tell Paul and Rodney what she had said.

"Aw, that's so much B.S. What does a cracker like that know about what it takes to make it in this neighborhood?"

"Yeah, who does that honky ho think she is? We're making it, aren't we?"

And I understood what they were saying. Compared to everyone else, Paul and Rodney were making it. Their dad was gone and their mama was real poor. There were nine kids in the family and they had to move all of them into a really tiny apartment over on Fountain, just two blocks from school. There was always rough stuff happening at their house. GIs stopping by to talk to their underage sisters, fighting, all kinds of drama. One of their older brothers had gone stone-cold crazy.

But Paul and Rodney always had bank and a girl and they could handle themselves in a fight. They were right. They were making it. Mrs. Beatty was full of B.S.

So things continued, business as usual.

Even though Rodney was two years older, he was going with a girl who was in seventh grade with Paul and me. She knew the ropes when it came to sex, so one day Rodney told us to skip class and bring her to their house and to have her bring two more girls with her. So we did.

Their family's apartment really was small. The kitchen was part of the living room and then there were just two tiny bedrooms. Three rooms all together—small, but still a good place to hang out. When we all got to the apartment, Rodney and Paul had no problem, but the girl I was with didn't want to give it up. So I went into the other bedroom and told Rodney's girl to go tell her to give it up.

Well, Rodney's girl went and talked to her alone for a few minutes. I never knew what she said or how she did it, but when I went back in, everything was just fine. I screwed her and then I left.

Paul was very private about his love life. That was a funny thing about him. No matter how strong we were with our cons and scams and no matter how tight we were in our fights (especially against the Mexicans who seemed to have a thing against us), Paul always kept his love life secret. I would try to get him to tell me about his girlfriend and what was going on, but he just wouldn't. So, I teased him a lot about that.

Even after Paul's family moved two blocks away from the school, and about a mile away from my house, he still walked over every morning to meet me and walk to school together. The only thing that changed was that now we met in a different place in the alley... a block or two closer to his side of the neighborhood.

And still, he was never late and so we were never late for school.

One day after school, Paul came by my house. He and Rodney, and their older brother, Michael, were in a car, a Cougar. They had come to pick me up to go riding with them. I wanted to go really bad and I could have gone anyway, but for some reason I went in to ask my mom if I could go. She said no and deep inside something told me to stick with that.

So I went back out to the alley where they were waiting. "I can't go. She said no."

Paul just smiled his big smile like he always did and said, "Okay. See you in the morning."

I don't know how I spent the rest of the evening, but I do know I woke up earlier than usual the next morning. It was kind of cold outside and I walked down to our meeting spot and waited. Paul never came.

I finally walked on to school, and man, was it different walking alone. I decided to stop by Paul's house to see what was going on. As I walked inside, I saw his mother and a lot of other people sitting and standing around crying. When they finally noticed I was there, it got real quiet. I heard somebody say, "He doesn't know. Ain't nobody told him yet." They made me sit down and began to tell me what happened.

Paul had been killed in a car accident, and Rodney and Michael were in Intensive Care. As it was described to me, they ran into a telephone pole at Fountain and Union, going about ninety miles an hour. It had always been a dangerous curve, way too sharp even if you were going slow.

I sat there for a while and they all seemed to feel sadder for me than for their loss. I watched them feeling things, but my mind was going in all different directions. I didn't know what to think or feel. For a long time I couldn't move my body. I guess I was in shock.

I went on to school. For the first time since knowing Paul, I was late.

When I got there, I went to the office to check in, so I wouldn't be marked absent. Everyone at the counter and in the immediate area just stared at me. I was in a daze and it probably showed.

Mrs. Beatty, came out and said, "Promise, I'm surprised you're here today after what has happened. Thank God you weren't in that car. Why don't you go home? You don't need to be here today."

I said, "I'm okay. I want to go to class." That whole day the daze never lifted, and later that week Rodney died.

The funeral home was right down the street. I went in to view the bodies. I was the first one there. Man, Paul looked strange lying there dead. I sat there for a long time and then people began to come in and look. I watched the different reactions and listened to the comments people made. But I still didn't have a reaction or comment of my own. I just looked. I felt like an island.

Finally, a girl came in and put a ring on his finger. I asked her who she was. It was Paul's girlfriend that he had kept so many secrets about. She knew everything about me, though. I felt sad for her. Her name was Brenda.

The funeral was held at a Catholic church downtown. I'll never forget how I ran all around town trying to find the place. I had never been there before and I just had an address. Once again, I got there first. Then the people began to arrive. Paul and Rodney's mother and family were escorted in and I followed behind them. They were seated on the front row and there was no more room left. So I sat on the next pew back. I just sat there. I couldn't believe my best friend, my brother, was dead.

Time came to go to the gravesite and I asked where it was. His mom told me their grave was in Denver. I didn't have a ride, so I just went home and said goodbye to Paul from there.

Paul was gone. I'd have to walk to school by myself, play by myself, laugh by myself, fight by myself. I was alone. All alone like an island.

AN ISLAND

Does an island need an ocean
In order to exist?

Can pebbles be shaped smooth
Without the beach's grist?

Can the sun be the sun
And not produce heat?

Does the sky need the stars
For it to be complete?

Can a rainbow come into being
When there's never been a rain?

Can a boy without a friend
Not suffer excruciating pain?

Does the island need the ocean
For them both to survive?

How does one go on
In a world filled with goodbyes?

Promise Lee

SIX

The men in my father's family have always had a strong addiction to women. There's a popular story—almost a legend—in our family about Great Granddad Solomon Jeffrey, my Dad's granddad, who was a carpenter. He was working on a roof one day when he suddenly let out a long yell and collapsed. The other men rushed to his aid and asked what was wrong.

"I'm dying!" he moaned.

"What can we do?" they asked.

"I need a woman. Get me a woman."

The men stopped working and went and found one for him. After that, he got up and finished the job. My granddad, his son, had affairs with eighteen- and twenty-year-old girls clear into his eighties.

I do believe in the reality of generational behaviors and curses.

When I was in kindergarten we lived in Japan, and I mostly spent time with a girl named Brigade. She was a year older than me and one of the few black kids in my American GI class. Brigade (I later wondered why someone would give a name like that to a daughter) would come and knock on my door and take me to the stairwell of our apartment building to "play." She had eyebrows that slanted toward her nose and she didn't smile much. She always wore a scowl on her face, so I felt like I had to do what she said.

One day when she came to get me, we headed for the roof. In the stairwell she stopped in front of me and told me to get on top of her like the men did to the women in the movies. When I laid down on her and her frowning face and mine were nose to nose, she ordered me to wiggle around and rub on her. Her face was hard and unfriendly.

"Look, you got to push your thing up and on my thing. That's the way to do it."

"That's the way to do what?"

"That's the way you be friends. Friends have secrets and this is the way grown-ups make secrets. Now you do what I say. Unzip your pants."

I still wasn't sure why my friend wanted me to do this. No words ran through my mind. But my queasy stomach and clouded thoughts made me know. I knew way deep down inside that some wrongdoing had been done to Brigade.

If rubbing my thing on her made Brigade feel as bad as it did me, why did she want me to do it? I just couldn't understand.

When I went home that afternoon, my mind stayed in the stairwell, and the uneasiness stayed in my gut. Bedtime was a welcome relief but my dreams tortured me. That was when I first dreamed that dream… being small and not being able to shake the smallness.

After my encounters with Brigade began, I became interested in the things men and women did together privately. And though I had never wondered about it before, I began to think that I did not have an understanding of the female body.

So one day when I was about six or seven and our babysitter, Ms. Sheppard, was ironing some shirts, I crawled over to where she was and, lying on my back, looked up her dress. This bubbly, brown-skinned woman was someone I loved and respected. When she took care of us, she was always kind and her face always wore a smile.

Under her long skirt, it was warm and musty smelling, but nothing in particular caught my interest. She didn't notice that I was there, so I decided maybe I could understand the mystery better if I touched it. What could be the harm if she wasn't paying attention? She would never know.

Her brown legs were dimpled and smooth. I reached my hand up to run it along the inside of her where it looked soft and inviting. When I did that, I learned something, but it had nothing to do with the female body.

Ms. Sheppard jumped, then looked down at me so startled and hurt. Then she just burst into tears. Really crying. Not yelling and screaming, but shaking and sobbing.

I stood up quickly and watched as she moved over to the couch to sit down with her face in her hands. My feet felt heavy and no matter how much I told them to walk over there to her, they just wouldn't. I stood there, silent, watching her for a long time, looking at the top of her head as she bent over, wishing she would look up with a big smile on her face and say, "Just kidding."

But she didn't. She just kept crying like her heart was broken.

I started to feel angry. I hadn't hit her, so why was she crying? I wanted to take it back just to make her stop. The more she cried, the worse I felt. I didn't know how to fix what I had done.

I was still standing there watching her when my father walked in with my mother trailing him. I still couldn't say anything. I didn't know *what* to say. Even after Ms. Sheppard had explained the whole thing to my parents, I still didn't open my mouth.

I never could say so, but I was ashamed for hurting her feelings. I was ashamed I had touched her in this way. When my father whipped me with his belt, I took my licks and didn't mind because I knew I had done wrong. I had hurt her.

All that evening, though, and even after bedtime, I kept thinking about Brigade. Thinking about *her* touches. Thinking about her mean-looking face.

I wondered if she ever felt sorry for making me feel the same way Ms. Sheppard felt. I wondered if she felt like Ms. Sheppard did when someone touched her. I wondered, *if I made her feel like Ms. Sheppard felt, why did she want me to rub on her?*

It was a funny thing. I loved Ms. Sheppard and, in a way, I loved Brigade, but touching them both just made me feel too bad.

I was thirteen. Walt Disney World was opening in Florida, but I wasn't going to see it any time soon or maybe ever. I was out explor-ing another world. Mom and Daddy were divorcing, so things weren't tight. They were doing their thing and I was doing mine. I would come home when I wanted to, sleep for a while, maybe show-er. Leave when I wanted to. Most of the time, I knew when they wouldn't be there. That's when I'd go by. In all, they knew they couldn't control me. They didn't even know how to try anymore.

Mom was just sick of his running around. I was sick of it, too. Partly because it hurt Mom, but also because ever since I was a little boy, Daddy had told me to leave those white girls alone; and all this mess was over him chasing white women. I never really understood why. I just figured it was one more reason to discount his advice and counsel. Instead, I figured he was holding out on me. That having lots of women was really the way to go.

I had been getting mixed messages from my father. I especially remember one time before they divorced, when I was about twelve. It was one of those summer nights when sleep just won't come. Skin sticks to skin and laying on your sheets feels like laying on the beach. Usually, there was at least a breeze, but this night everything was as still as it was quiet.

My mother appeared in our bedroom doorway and said, "Come on y'all. We're going for a ride." My eight-year-old sister, Gina, was already up, but the four of us boys pulled on our jeans and gladly loaded ourselves into the station wagon.

It seemed just a little strange that on such a quiet, lazy evening Mom pulled out of the driveway with a screech, but the feeling of the cool night air on my damp skin made me forget all about it.

We drove for a long time, past where houses came in rows and long past the frequent corner gas stations. The farther we went, the more fields and wide open spaces we passed. Finally, we pulled into the driveway of a house, just like we lived there. "Promise Yul, go up to the door and get your Daddy."

I was surprised at what Mom said because I didn't know we were going to pick up Daddy. I just thought we were taking a ride. But being the oldest—the man—I knocked on the door anyway. A pretty white woman opened it. She didn't say anything like, "Yes?" or "Can I help you?" She just stood there. Then I looked past her and saw Daddy sitting up in the living room, just as comfortable as you please, watching TV. Then I knew. And I always knew after that.

So Daddy came home with us that night, but it was never the same. I had learned that words are just words, but you watch actions to know the truth. The part I hadn't learned was to stand back and watch my actions. I guess I was just too angry and too young.

I had left home. Shortly after the shooting, Mom and Daddy had divorced. Mom remarried. I was living between both of their houses, but mostly at Dad's and on the street. Needles shot through my stomach, reminding me that I hadn't eaten for... well, for a long time. Living between friends' houses and the street never guaranteed you a meal. So a friend of mine named Archie and I headed over to the King Soopers to see what we could take, and I found much more than I expected.

I wouldn't have used the word steal because stealing implies stealth and secrecy, and we had no intention of sneaking around. We were hungry and the grocery store was the logical place to get food. Boldy and with pride. We strolled into the store, picked up some bologna and some cheese, and strolled out.

It was a beautiful night and the prospect of a meal made it more so. But these thoughts were interrupted by an unfamiliar voice shouting, "Hey! Stop right there!"

I cast a nonchalant glance over my shoulder. My mouth answered, "What?" but my eyes registered, "WHAT?"

There before me stood the most indescribable, melt-in-your-mouth, brown-butter-skinned, pearl-toothed, dazzle-smiled, sparkley-eyed beauty my heart had ever pounded after. If we had paid for the stuff, I surely would have checked out *this* checker.

"You want to bring that stuff back here before I have to come and get you?"

Then, intending a double meaning, I answered, "Come and get me? You think you can catch me?" And in a sheer act of the will, I turned and walked away.

Archie and I had gotten all the way to the end of the building when (luckily) she grabbed me. "Look," I explained, "We need something to eat. That's why we got the stuff."

"Oh, you do, do you? What about getting supper from your mama?" She spoke with a New York accent that completely sent me over the top.

"Mama! I'm eighteen years old." I lied through my thirteen-year-old teeth.

"Really? Me, too," she lied through her twenty-four-year-old teeth. "Look, I have to go back to work now, but my name's Iris. Come and see me sometime. My apartment's right over there," and she pointed across the street.

A few days later I went to see her. She had a little baby. But we would still enjoy sitting around together spending time. She just took me in. I wasn't going to school, so I would just hang out and drink Mad Dog 20/20 all day. When that happened, she'd always say the same thing, "I know how to sober you up."

And no matter how it went down, it would almost always be just like she said. She'd work that booze right out of my system. But sometimes that Mad Dog was a stronger lover than even that beautiful girl. At those times, it didn't bring on a rising in my groin. It brought on a rage rising from deep down in my soul. Then, plain and simple, I beat the hell out of her.

Her brother had brought her to Colorado Springs from New York and he felt responsible for her. That's why he'd always come by and try to convince her I was just a hoodlum. He never knew I beat her, but he could tell just by looking at me that I was up to no good.

The first time I slept with her I noticed the big scar that ran completely around her body, but I never asked her about it. I recall sitting on her couch with my buddies one day. Iris had gotten up to get us some drinks and when she was gone, one of my buddies said, "Hey man, she's crippled."

"Naw," I said.

"Yeah, she just doesn't have a big shoe on. She wears one of those big shoes."

No, she had never worn a big shoe, at least not around me. Although maybe she could have. But the point was, I had never asked her about that either. I just thought the limp was her way of walking sexy.

And even though I mostly lived with Iris, my mom still kept up with me. And from her own experience, she didn't have to guess about anything. She knew what was going on. So for Iris's sake, my mom bought her and her baby an airline ticket back East. Neither mom nor Iris ever told me this, but I always knew.

I went to the airport with her and as I watched the plane taxi away, I remembered sleeping with her, and as the plane took off and took her away forever, I ached with an endless pain, deep in my heart. Somewhere inside, I knew she was flying away just like the little bee so long ago. She was just keeping the stinger that for some reason I had tried to take from her.

So I watched, helpless, as she flew out of my life. I'm sorry, Iris. I really loved you.

Iris actually found her way back to the Springs some six or nine months later. When she came back, I spent some time with her, but she ended up with someone else. When she'd flown off, I began to put Daddy's philosophy into action. I had girlfriends from Fountain and Widefield (small nearby suburbs) to the farthest reaches of Colorado Springs. In fact, I kept a list of all the girls I wanted from school, from the neighborhood, from church, friends of friends, every possible source. Every one of them I'd slept with had a check by her name. It was a game. Like taking food from the grocery store. Getting what you wanted, getting what you needed.

Mostly I still lived on the streets, but every now and then I'd go home for a few days. It was always nice then. Mom would often be at Daddy's house and pet me a little to try to make me want to stay. Daddy would try to impart some wisdom to me. It was okay for a little while.

They never interfered with me making my list. Every day and every night I'd be out with my girls, persuading them as my childhood friend Brigade had persuaded me, to visit some secluded place far away from parents or other intruders. Sometimes I'd press them up against the wall of the garage or grab them from behind in a backyard shed or slip into a closet with them. It didn't really matter where, so long as I checked them off of my list. Sometimes I'd visit them at their house and just wait for their mom and dad to go to bed. Then I got the chance to screw them on the couch or some other out-of-the-way place. Or on occasion, I wouldn't add any check marks to my list at all. I'd just enjoy the girl's company.

No matter what part of town I was in, I'd find myself at midnight or 1:00 in the morning running across some field headed back to the Southside. And always, always I'd be running like hell, scared to death I'd step in a hole or get bit by a snake.

One time, when I was home for a visit, my mom decided to clean out the top shelf of the closet of the room where I was staying. And she found it. She found the list.

Now my mom was pretty street smart, so she asked me about it. And me, knowing she was pretty street smart and even being the con I was, I couldn't put any kind of an answer together that made any sense. I stuttered and stammered and finally her eyes just flashed like fire, and she turned around and walked away from me.

"You lowdown, nasty little man-child... Just like your daddy."

She never said anything more about it and neither she nor Daddy tried to discipline me in any way. The only thing that happened was that my mom's sister, Tena, sat me down the next day and explained to me about condoms and V.D. and a bunch more stuff I just partly ignored.

Always, when I was running, I'd be on the lookout for some of that Mad Dog or weed or speed or acid. You see, a lot of the time I spent with my girls, I'd be feeling good on a number of scores. Then it would be just like with Iris. Either they'd screw the booze and dope out of me or I'd wind up pounding their faces in.

But even when I beat them bad, they always let me come back. That's because getting beat up was just like home for lots of my girls. One girl I knew was from a whole family of prostitutes. The daddy pimped the mom *and* the daughters. Some of my girls saw their moms take it hard from boyfriends or husbands, if they had them. Life was hard for all of them—for us all!

Even knowing this about my girls, I didn't take the care I needed to not hurt them more. I knew the drugs and booze stirred up all the fight that was in me... and I consumed them anyway. And afterward, I couldn't remember it happening until I saw them. And then, when I'd look at those beautiful faces all lumpy and purple, I would know it was me who had done it.

And I'd be so sorry.
But I couldn't stop.

SEVEN

It was another Mad Dog day. Drugs, booze, and sex had become a big part of my life. By three in the afternoon, my friends and I had smoked a half lid of weed and drunk almost four bottles of orange Mad Dog wine. I had been in and out of Pikes Peak Park two times, visiting girlfriends. Finally, I ended up at the Hunt, just hanging out.

"Hey, Terrell!" I yelled.

He sped by in a yellow Vega station wagon filled with girls. He saw me and they made the block.

"What it is, man?" Terrell asked impatiently.

"Where you going with all this meat?"

"Nowhere. Just ridin'."

One of the girls in the back spoke up and in a throaty-sweet voice asked, "Where you *want* to go?"

Stoned as I was, I could still feel my heart start to pound with that coy invitation kind of question.

"With you, baby girl," I whined, throwing that desperate, pleading kind of tone in on top.

Terrell interrupted, getting to the point, "Let me drop this dead weight off and we'll be back. Where you gonna be? Here?"

"No, pick me up at the lake and bring me some MD orange."

Forty-five minutes later the yellow Vega cruised the lake. This time there was just Alice and her sister and Terrell in the car.

The sun was just starting to set. And in the soft dusky light of evening, Alice's skin was like satin. Tones of light and dark shimmered together, casting shadows and mystery over all her features. I climbed into the back, sweaty palms and all, and then over the backseat into the cargo area and my waiting beauty. By the time we hit the interstate going north toward Denver, we were busy getting to know each other.

Terrell and Alice's sister, Shawna, were kind of quiet, listening to our goings-on. I knew they had wanted to get into the back. So I said, "Pull over and let me piss."

As I stood on the side of the road, I closed my eyes and let it flow. I could feel myself rocking back on my heels and I enjoyed my brain spinning inside my head. "God!" I thought, "I feel good." I finished, but neglected to close my pants. Vaguely I thought this might score me some attention.

When I got close to the car, I saw that Terrell and Shawna were in fact in the back and Alice was in the front. I shrugged. That was cool.

I got into the driver's seat, put the car in gear and asked, "Where we goin'?"

From the back I heard a cheerful cry, "Denver. Let's have some fun!" So I pulled onto the highway and continued heading north.

I had only driven about five miles when I saw the flashing lights of a police car behind me. I maneuvered the car off the road and waited. The cops finally came to my window, took one whiff and said, "Get out of the car."

I stumbled even in this endeavor. "We've gotten at least a dozen calls reporting your swerving for twenty miles or more. Where's your license?"

I was thirteen years old. I had no license and I didn't think I had been swerving at all. So I said nothing.

"How old are you then? What's your name?"

"I'm Thomas Johnson. I'm seventeen."

"You're going to jail, son." He started to load me into the back of his car, but then let me take a minute to give my money to Terrell.

"Follow us and get me out on bond," I instructed him.

They drove me to the Castle Rock jail and once there, they walked me down the hall to the only cell they had. There was only one other guy in there, a wino. They locked me in and I slept like a baby.

The next day they brought me to court and told me I could have a trial or go before the judge. I looked closely at the judge and figured he would be my best chance. Maybe I could con him and he'd let me go. Well, to my surprise he didn't buy anything I had to say. He told me I could pay a fine or do time.

Since Terrell had all my money and since I wasn't living at home and couldn't call my folks, I took the twenty-one-day sentence, cursing the whole time. The whole thing took a few minutes, and the same officer who brought me to court escorted me back to the cell where I sat and sat and sat.

Terrell never showed up.

Bull Durham tobacco was issued to the prisoners for rolling cigarettes. On the first day I gave mine to the wino. By the second day I was so bored, I decided to take up smoking just to have something to do besides look at the walls. I was good at rolling weed already, but this gave me time to perfect my technique. Somewhere a long time ago, I had heard that you could get high from smoking orange peelings. So, one day when I got the chance I tried that. It didn't work, so I looked at the walls some more.

On another day I tried to take a shower, but the single stall was so dark and isolated, I decided it was better to be dirty. And I sat and sat and sat.

For nearly three weeks, this was the sum total of what I did in the Castle Rock jail.

All the time I sat in Castle Rock rotting, I thought about Terrell and why he didn't come. Terrell and I went back a long, long way.

Just a few months before, he and I were riding around in a Dodge Roadrunner with two soldiers who were a lot older than us. One of them was dating Terrell's older sister. The four of us had been smoking so much weed that the smoke blocked our vision from the back to the front seat of the car. As we cruised the red light district of Nevada Avenue, we stopped at the Platte Street traffic light right next to a car full of rednecks. They were flipping us the finger and spitting chewing tobacco juice at us and calling us niggers.

I was sitting in the back seat, looking at the bulgy-eyed, hideous, red face with the veins straining out of its neck and wondering why no one in our car was even responding. When the light changed, we sped far ahead of them and I thought that was the end of it, but not three or four minutes later they pulled up alongside of us again when we stopped at Cimmaron. This time they started hitting the

Roadrunner with baseball bats.

I wasn't afraid, just pissed. "What's the matter with y'all," I yelled at Terrell and the soldiers.

"Look under my seat," the driver instructed.

When I slid my hand beneath the seat I felt a steel pipe. But as I pulled it out farther and saw the wooden handle, I realized it was actually a sawed-off shotgun. I gripped it in my hands.

Immediately I rolled down the car window, spit at the rednecks and flipped them the finger. Then we sped up again, leaving them behind for a moment.

As expected, a few seconds later they were beside us again, still carrying on. This time I smiled at them showing all my teeth. I aimed the shotgun and without a minute's hesitation, pulled the trigger.

Their faces went white, like the Klan sheets they probably had in their trunk. After I fired on them, we sped off.

They never caught up with us again, but the night wasn't over for me, Terrell, or the two soldiers. We drove farther down Highway 115, smoking dope until we couldn't see each other for all the smoke.

For some reason, the soldier who was driving decided to take the turn onto Fort Carson. As we inched along toward the guardhouse that would gain us entrance to the fort, Terrell said, "Roll the windows down before we get there."

When we did, there was so much smoke pouring out, I'm sure it looked like the car was on fire.

Without even speaking with us, the Military Police pulled the car over at the gate and radioed for backup. Before we knew it, there were MPs everywhere. I was so stoned, all those pigs didn't even blow my high.

They took Terrell and me to separate rooms to question us. "I'm sixteen, I told you. My name is Eddy James and I live at 1612 Hemlock Court."

Of course, every word out of my mouth was a lie, but Terrell told the truth. Finally, I gave them an address close to Terrell's and they loaded us into the car to take us home. We were just kids, but the soldiers we were with, we found out later, were wanted for murder and for being AWOL.

When the MPs pulled up in front of Terrell's house to take him in and talk to his mama, I jumped out of the car and made a run for it. I jumped a few fences and headed up the alley. They never did catch me and my folks never found out. Terrell and I have laughed about that whole evening, the rednecks and the MPs, many times since.

Yeah, there had been some good times between us. But this was not a good time. Damn that Terrell. Where was he? Friendship or not, I would have to beat him down. I was mad, plus my rep was on the line. I had let him take something from me. No way could I return to the streets without teaching him a lesson. But mostly I was mad.

Twenty days had passed. I was filthy. I was sick of smoking. The wino made me want to puke. And I couldn't wait to get my hands on Terrell.

"Lee, you got a visitor," I heard a guard call.

This better be Terrell, I thought. Instead, who should be walking along behind the guard, but Uncle Bud and another fellow I'll never forget, by the name of Don Ritchie. Two of the greatest men in the world to me.

"Mr. Dunlap, what are you doing here?"

"I heard on the street that you probably needed some help."

"Man, I'm ready to get out of here."

"Promise, how long have you been here?"

"About three weeks."

"Why didn't your folks come for you?"

"'Cause they don't know I'm here. Besides, I can't call 'em now. I'll be in deep trouble."

Uncle Bud and Don got me out and took me back to the Springs. They didn't take me home, though. Uncle Bud called my mom and let her know I was okay.

"I'm going to beat that boy 'til he can't sit down," she screamed into the phone.

"Well, Mrs. Lee, as upset as you are, maybe I should just keep him here for a while. Just until you cool down," he told her.

And he kept his word. I stayed at his house for a while and luckily, this kept my mom from taking my life or at least my hide.

Terrell wasn't so lucky. I found out he had used my money that very night to buy a bag of weed and just left me there on purpose. When I caught him, I beat him up real bad. And when I had him down, I grabbed his nappy fro and pulled his head back and told him, "I ought to cut all your hair off."

This is what my daddy used to say to me when I was in trouble. Maybe I should have actually done it. Maybe Daddy should have actually done it. Maybe I wouldn't have ended up in so much trouble.

Yeah, I had stayed in jail all that time and my folks had never known. Mostly, it was because I was living here and there. On the streets, with Iris, staying at friends' houses, sometimes at home.

So, somewhere along the line, when I was about fourteen, the court agreed to put me in foster placement, assigning me to an Air Force Airman, Hason, who had volunteered for the job. Boy, were they snowed.

Hason was perhaps seven or eight years my senior. He lived in a house with lots of other military guys, Army and Air Force. There was Keith and Slam who were big time wrestlers. There was JJ and Jimmy Long. And of course, Wash (short for Washington), who always let me use his car.

Originally, I met them selling dope. But the big racket while I lived there was with the stuff I stole. Someone would always say, "Hey, Li'l Brother, can you get me a tape deck?" or something like that. Then the next day, I'd steal a tape deck and sell it to them. Sometimes they'd keep it. Sometimes they'd sell it.

They'd always let me and my friend Larry White hang around while they were partying. We'd crash out one day and the next day and the next day and the next day, just laying around stoned for days and days at a time. We mostly always had plenty of drugs around, but when we didn't, Larry and I would go to the 7-Eleven and steal Robitussin or Formula 44. It was some potent stuff. You drank a bottle of that and it was a high just like heroine. You'd be nodding. I suppose I stayed high because I enjoyed the feeling. Now that I look back, it was a way to medicate. I now know while I was medicating, it prevented me from meditating. If one doesn't take time to think, they sink. And I did.

We mostly used what we called Electric Kool-Aid. All we'd do is mix up regular Kool-Aid with lots and lots of sugar. Then we would add some hits of windowpane acid. Much of the acid would crystallize at the bottom with the sugar, but some of it would dissolve. It was a great way to get high.

Everybody in the house loved Kool-Aid, electric or not. It was a staple, especially with a lot of sugar in it. But Slam loved the Kool-Aid more than anybody else.

Whenever anybody called out, "Who drank all the Kool-Aid?" Slam would always say, "I drunk it."

Then we'd ask, "So why didn't you make some more?"

"I did," he'd say.

So then we'd have to ask, "Well, where is it?"

And then he'd always say the same dumb thing again, "I drunk it."

Once we mixed up some of that Electric Kool-Aid and decided to make it supersonic. So we put in twenty or maybe thirty hits of windowpane. Then Larry came by and said, "Hey man, come on. Let's get out of here."

So I put the Kool-Aid in the refrigerator and left. I didn't think about the consequences. While we were gone, it began to snow. A storm had moved in and the temperature had really dropped. It wasn't fit for man nor beast outdoors, so we cut our carousing short after a few hours and went back to the house.

When we got there all the windows were wide open. It was freezing and the snow was blowing into the house, half piled up and half melted on the window ledges. Opening the door created a huge draft and all kinds of papers were swirling down to the floor from the counters and tables as we walked in.

I saw Slam sitting on the sofa.

"Man what are you doing? It's freezing in here!" I yelled.

To my surprise he said, "I am the son of Malcolm X."

"What? Fool, close the windows."

"I am the spirit of Martin."

"Slam! Are you crazy? Get up and help me close the windows."

Larry and I looked at each other. "Man, he's just trippin'."

We shook our heads and proceeded to shut the windows and clear up the mess of papers that was everywhere. I gathered up a bunch of them and took them to the kitchen counter to file them into a neat stack. I was working methodically when I looked up and noticed the empty Kool-Aid pitcher on the counter.

My jaw dropped open and I thought I might puke. I looked over at Slam. He was still staring straight ahead and talking on and on about Malcolm, Martin, and lots of other black heroes.

The other guys came home and all of us worked real hard trying to get Slam to snap out of it. But after three days we knew it was over. He was in the Air Force and had missed work. Everyone knew they had to take him in. When they finally did, they admitted him immediately to the State Mental Hospital. He was gone... he had lost his mind... all that acid... he had lost his mind. What I did to Slam is one of the biggest regrets of my life, though at the time, I just thought it was too bad.

Shortly after that I quit living with the GIs. They were okay, but none of the brothers in the neighborhood could compete. The GIs always had money and cars and could come into the neighborhood and get all the women. So there was a deep rivalry there. In the end, I knew I was a Southsider, not a GI. So I came back to the hood to live.

I guess it was a good thing I did because eventually the brothers shot up the place where the GIs lived. Just sprayed it with bullets. I never knew *exactly* who did it, but everyone knew it was Southsiders.

I heard that Slam was starting to do a lot better, so I hitchhiked down to Pueblo to the state hospital to see him.

"Hey, Slam. How you doin'? You remember me?"

"Yeah."

"What's my name, Slam?"

"Yeah."

What's *your* name, Slam?"

"Yeah."

Yeah, Slam went crazy, and the brothers went crazy, and the foster care system went crazy, and Mom and Daddy went crazy. Everyone went crazy.

EIGHT

Earlier that year, my folks had decided to have me go live with Mom's sisters, Maxine and Tena, in Los Angeles. The goal was to get me away from the influences here. To give me a fresh start before I, as Mom put it, "went completely bad."

I was eager for the change. I had seen Los Angeles on TV and in magazines and it seemed like the place I wanted to be. It was full of the rich and famous and swarming with danger. People went to find fame and fortune on the streets of Los Angeles. That's just what I wanted to do.

So my brother Charmas and I boarded the plane in Colorado Springs and had an uneventful flight all the way to L.A.

Now Aunt Tena was the youngest of my mom's sisters and just as sweet as could be. But it was Aunt Maxine who was at the airport waiting for us. She was little and short and could whip an elephant if she took a mind to do it. Before she even said hello, she announced, "I hope y'all didn't bring no roaches wit ya."

Charmas responded by saying, "Hi, Aunt Maxine," and giving her a big hug.

My response was to just stand there, puzzled over the roach thing. I had never actually seen a roach in Colorado. I guess the altitude was too high and climate too dry and cold for them, unless you're really filthy. We made jokes like, "Your mama got roaches in her house," and stuff like that but I had never actually seen one before.

But sure enough, when we pulled up to her house, she took out our suitcases and dumped them all out onto the driveway. Right in front of the house, in front of the neighbors, she shook out our clothes, underwear and all. She was dead serious about the roaches.

Luckily, Janice and Victor, Maxine's kids, our cousins, came out of the house just then. Maxine kept her kids pretty sheltered. Janice was very beautiful and Victor was well groomed, too.

It didn't take me long to size up the situation with my aunts. Maxine was married and lived in a house near 74th and Compton. She was tough and kept everything in order, including her kids. Around her I always had the impression that I was there to protect her sheltered children from the elements of their own neighborhood. I was intelligent, good looking, quick witted, polite (when I wanted to be) and spoke properly. I was "presentable" to company and I had a role to fulfill.

Aunt Tena was not married but had a daughter, my cousin Sharon. They lived in a little apartment that had lots of gangs around it. Sharon seemed real quiet but really she had just learned how to maintain and not be affected by all the craziness going on in the streets. She knew how to just walk straight on and avoid problems, no matter what. Aunt Tena would say to me, "Promise Yul, it's rough out here. Stay away from trouble, but if it comes to you, protect yourself."

It was also tough where Aunt Maxine lived. Aunt Tena believed in giving us some life skills (before the term was even popular) to help us along. She taught us a little cooking and cleaning, that kind of stuff. But even before that, she told Sharon to teach us how to ride the bus. Soon I could ride the bus all over L.A. with my eyes closed and still know which stop was which, just by listening to the sounds of the city. And I had never seen so much action in all my life. There was every sort of person: rich, poor, every nationality. And they all dressed different than people in Colorado because the weather was so good. And the music! So many soul stations on the radio and sounds I had never heard in Colorado. Colorado Springs didn't have *any*.

On the other hand, Aunt Maxine ordered us tailor-made clothes, enrolled us in summer school, and signed us up to sing in the local church choir. Her plan was to keep us so busy we wouldn't have time for gangs.

Thus the stage was set for my double life.

During those first few days of summer, I got my bearings and sized up my living situation. I preferred to stay with Aunt Tena, but mostly Charmas and I lived with Maxine. So every day I went to summer school.

It wasn't too bad, though, because it gave me the chance to meet some people. One of the first was Cindy, a white girl, older than me.

One day, out of the blue she said, "I've seen you ride the bus. I'd like to know if you'd ride the bus home with me."

As sharp as I thought I was, I didn't pick up her not-so-hidden meaning and asked completely innocently, "What bus do you take?"

"The number ten," she said. "Come on."

So I went and we stopped at some apartments along the way. She took me into the complex's washeteria and before I even knew what was going on, she had ahold of me and was, as I saw it, trying to rape me. It was a Brigade flashback.

I grabbed her wrist and began to twist it. I steeled my eyes directly into hers.

"Wait a minute," she stuttered. "I was just kidding."

I shoved her away from me, against the dryers, and left.

On the way home, I decided to let it slide. But a few mornings later I got to school and there she was standing on the steps. The school doors weren't open yet. As always, the busses had gotten us there early.

"Want to get high?" she called from the steps.

I looked at her for a minute without answering. "Okay," I said a little reserved, "What you got?"

"Some pot. It's at my friend's house."

So we went over to the friend's house and went into the garage. Even in the morning hours it was sweltering hot. It was a true California garage with surfboards hanging up all over the place.

She lit a joint and handed it to me, smiling. I took a toke and decided to bogart it, for a test. She didn't say anything, so after a while I passed it back to her.

The sweat was rolling down the side of my face and chest. My jeans were getting damp. Damn, it was hot in there.

But the pot was good. And so when she showed me she was interested, all I could do was give her what she wanted. Then I left, high, and went back to school.

My social life was coming along just fine.

Coming out of Maxine's early in the morning for school was always the same. The smog would be hanging low and thick around your throat. There'd be people noises, but nothing like birds or insects or any nature kind of things. The heat would already be closing in. All around you would be the smell of car fumes.

On one such fine morning, I chanced to look across the way to Maxine's neighbors. The family had a daughter and a set of sixteen-year-old twin boys. I had gotten to know the twins because they were so puzzling to me. One of them was huge like a monster—tall, wide, thick, and hairy. The other was like an elf. He was little, but that's not all. His face was cartoonish. I called him Goblin.

The twins were standing on the front porch, smoking a joint. I was curious, though, because it couldn't be weed. The joint was too skinny. I got closer, stepping up onto their porch.

My eyes scanned nervously for Maxine, "Let me have a hit."

"You sure? This ain't weed," the monster said.

"Man, pass it to me."

I hit it hard. It was almost minty or maybe herbal tasting.

"Here," I said, passing it back.

I noticed that they were both staring at me. Then BAM…I was whacked out. Angel Dust. PCP. I wanted another hit. On second thought, I just wanted to enjoy the high I had. I felt great.

Maxine never knew and couldn't tell when I was high. So Monster, Goblin, and I met almost every morning and my drug cabinet grew. Mom had sent some money with us and I spent it wisely. In Colorado Springs I had access to uppers and downers and all kinds of stuff, but it was expensive. Here I could get a roll (two) of reds for seventy-five cents. And they were potent. They became a staple of mine also.

"Want to go to the park?" Goblin called from across the driveway.

"Sure. Let's go." I wanted to play some basketball at the rec center which was part of the park. We were hanging close these days, so we had our routine.

"Don't smoke too much. Don't smoke too much." Goblin kept saying as I toked on that PCP. But I just ignored him.

By the time we got to the basketball court, I was completely whacked, but ready for a confrontation. And there, in every corner of the gym, were gangs marking out their space.

We walked around for a while and I was just hoping someone would say something to me or bump me. Then I'd be ready for action. But nothing happened inside. I guess they knew I was too high or too new or something. So Goblin and I walked outside again.

Once outside, I knew my time had come. There were a couple of guys dressed just alike: blue jeans cuffed over at the bottom with sharp creases down the front and white, white t-shirts tucked in real tight. They seemed so uniform. They were sharp.

"Hey, nig, Eastside here. What you claimin'?"

I said, "I ain't claimin' nothin'."

Then, with casual arrogance, he strolled toward me. "You got to claim something or get T-rolled.

"Look, man, I ain't claiming nothing but me. I ain't got time for that. So get on," I said.

"You got to fight whether you claim or not."

"Who do I have to fight?" I asked, sizing him up.

"Small Dog," he said, nodding toward one of the guys forming the circle. Small Dog wasn't so small. He had muscles everywhere and was both stocky and tall.

I glanced over and figured I could kick Small Dog's butt... if I hit him quick, hard and a lot of times. If I wanted to be left alone, I'd have to hurt him.

Six pairs of cuffed blue jeans circled around me and six pairs of biceps flexed inside their t-shirt sleeves. Small Dog moved forward, inside the circle.

I jumped to a karate stance and assumed an attitude hoping to bluff him, but he continued to move forward.

I connected first, a left to his head. Then I grabbed him in a headlock. From this position, though, he was able to pick me up and slam me to the ground so hard I lost my wind.

"Get up, school boy."

I took my time getting back on my feet, wondering the whole while why he didn't just stomp me to death.

We squared off again. This time I made sure he couldn't grab me. This time I boxed.

And I boxed his ears off.

Finally, the blue jeans moved in to break it up.

"Okay, nigga. We letting you go. But you better not claim nothing and if we need you, you better be ready to fall in."

I had wanted the confrontation, but was happy to be finished. The boxing lessons at the Boys' Club and on the streets of Colorado Springs paid off... probably saved my life, but I tell you—I was happy it was over.

That summer away from home, what I missed the most was my Mad Dog 20/20. She was my lover. And just like with a lover, I had to find another.

Yes, eventually Olde English 800 came to replace my MD. She was beautiful.

And just like the breasts on girls, I could take my choice of sizes. I came to love the twenty-ounce cans... plenty there for ecstasy. Even one could put you on your butt, just like a good piece of trim.

So one day, while I was out, I smoked some sherm, dropped some reds and loaded up on my O.E. 800. I became completely out of control. More out of control than I had ever been in my life. I tried to read the street signs to find my way back home to Maxine's, but my vision was blurred and double. My guts were churning. I struggled to maintain consciousness, but lost the fight.

Goose bumps stood rigid all over my body, but I couldn't pull my eyes open. My mind was swimming in and out of reality. Sometimes I would wake up with my arms and legs gyrating and sometimes I would wake up writhing and puking.

Without knowing how, but by the grace of God, I had made it back to Maxine's. Now she and Tena leaned over me. I was in the bathtub, stark naked, covered in ice. They were working like hell trying to revive me.

Sometimes, when I came to, I would hear them talking about

whether or not to call Mom. And sometimes I would hear them cry.

Aunt Maxine told me on the day I arrived in L.A. that if I wanted to stay permanently, I would have to keep out of trouble.

In my double life, I had attended church, summer school, and sung in the choir. But I had also gotten high, fought, and screwed more than ever.

Maxine and Tena had believed in me. I had visited Compton High School to look into permanent enrollment. Tena's boyfriend had taken Charmas and me to the Olympic trials that year. And, overall, I had tried to maintain a good standing, as much as for my mom's sake as for my aunts'.

But I had also visited the old shot-up house of the Symbionese Liberation Army, hung with Crips and Bloods and all kinds of gangs, and beaten up an old faggot who tried to seduce me in a public restroom. It was, indeed, a double life. But for Tena and Maxine, this was the end. They couldn't risk me getting myself killed. So as summer came to a close, I returned to Colorado Springs... older, street smarter, but no wiser than before. I say no wiser because I define wisdom as the appropriate application of knowledge.

NINE

I was back. Summer was coming to a close and September had already started. Life was good. Yeah, I was a man now. Fifteen years old and living on my own, in my own apartment. Yes, thanks to Mom, everything had worked out just right. Mom was married to Jimmy Dumas and they were stationed overseas. But when Mom heard about all the trouble I'd been in while I'd been living in L.A, they came to Colorado Springs to check on me.

Of course, she only knew about the stuff on my rap sheet. She didn't know anything about Hocking, who I'd shot two days before, or any of the other hundred things I'd never got caught for. If she had, she would have been here lots sooner.

They rented a real nice little place in the Londonderry apartment complex, so they'd have somewhere to stay while Mom figured out what was really going on with me. Now, my mom is sharp, but persuading her that I was going to be okay seemed to be all she needed. So I put on all my charm and told her what she wanted to hear.

In the end, they stayed for a month or two and then returned to Germany. And when they went, they put me in charge of their apartment until the lease was up the following month. Yes, everything had worked out just right.

So, being a man and having my own apartment, I had naturally invited some women—some knowledgeable women—over to keep me company.

They were due to arrive at my place at about 4:00 p.m., so I knew I had just enough time to get ready for them when my friend dropped me off that afternoon at my crib.

"Will you be out tonight?" he asked.

"If I have my way about it, I won't be out for a long time," I chuckled, thinking about the girls and how much fun I was going to have.

"Okay. See ya."

I shut the car door and was struck by how quiet and slow everything seemed. I was moving at a normal speed, but everything else seemed frozen, like in the *Twilight Zone*. Any other day there would have been lots of cars coming and going, people in the hallways, the sounds of little kids yelling and playing. But today there was nothing. Even the walls seemed to be watching me.

I opened my door and locked it behind me. Even in the crib something just wasn't quite right. I looked around the room for a clue and before I could find anything, my eyes fell on the clock. It was 3:45 p.m.! I had to get ready.

Quickly, I gathered up dirty dishes and pizza boxes as I slipped off my shoes. I pulled my shirt off over my head while I glanced into the bathroom to make sure there was nothing too nasty in there. And I added my pants to the pile of other laundry I threw on the floor of the closet, being careful to close the door behind me.

There, I was almost ready… naked except for my red silk boxers… crib relatively clean… all I needed was some ambience. I headed for the turntable I had acquired in a burglary the day before, but before I could get to it, I heard a knock at the door.

Usually, I was the one who arrived early, but this time the girls did.

I could feel myself get macho and cool as I walked toward the door.

"Who is it?"

They didn't answer and that made me even more eager. Beautiful girls who knew all the right moves, but played it coy. Hmm… I couldn't wait! I thought I heard a giggle. Immediately I unlocked the door and pulled it all the way open.

To my surprise, I found myself in my underwear facing a half-dozen pigs with guns.

A wave of fear ran through me until I recalled the turntable. The fact that I had shot Daniel Hocking two days before wasn't even on my mind. Of course, that was why they were there. I'd just go downtown and probably have to spend a night in juvenile detention. I'd have to return the turntable, but I'd be back home in a day. No big thing. After all, I was a juvenile.

But before I could really complete my thoughts, a size-twelve boot caught me right in the chest. I flew backward onto the floor, the wind knocked out of me. All around me were gun barrels and all I could think of was, *All this for a dumb turntable?*

"You're under arrest. Come with us."

"What for?"

"Don't worry about it. Just get your clothes on and come with us."

They cuffed my hands behind my back and escorted me down the hall. Now there was nothing quiet at all about the Londonderry Apartments. Every possible person was sticking their head out the door, hanging out in the hallway, or standing around in the parking lot.

I was put into the back of the police car and we drove off. On the way out, I saw the girls walking toward my building. This was one night there'd be no fun. I was sure of that. They would probably go on up to the apartment and I wouldn't be there, but the turntable would.

By the time we pulled up to the Zeb Pike Juvenile Detention Center, it was almost dark and I was still in the dark. What was I charged with? Who knew? Somehow, shooting Daniel Hocking had slipped my mind.

They directed me down the corridors to a cement room and locked me in. But not before I heard Larry's voice above the deafening quiet.

"Promise, is that you?"

I said, "Yeah, it's me." Then everything started to come together.

"Is Darrell here?

"Yeah, he's here. He's the one they picked up first."

Now everything made sense. Once before, Darrell and I had pulled a job. We had stolen some three-wheel all-terrain vehicles from the school district and rode all night long. We had a blast and when we were done, we stashed them in Darrell's basement. But at school the very next day, first thing, I was called to the principal's office. They had gotten to Darrell first and he had spilled his guts.

The same thing had happened now. This wasn't about a turntable or a burglary or any other thing. It was about our deal with Hocking. Darrell had sold us out.

I called his name, but he didn't answer.

The next day they transferred Larry and me over to the county jail for holding. Darrell came a couple of days later. They made a mistake and put him in a holding cell directly across from our cell-block, even though it wasn't until a few days later that Larry and I realized he was there.

It was feeding time and trays were being passed through the slits in the doors. I was looking through the peephole and saw his eyes looking out of the peephole in his door, directly across from mine. He jumped back. But I told Larry to come and look anyway. The very next day they moved him over on the other side... out of our sight.

Doing time in the county jail was the worst kind of time to do. There was no daylight. No windows. No library. Just TV and what-ever else you could think of to amuse yourself. Luckily, it wasn't as difficult to amuse yourself there as other places. That was mostly because of the setup. In every cellblock there was a dayroom and in every dayroom there was a TV and steel tables that you could sit around. There was also a shower stall with walls on three sides and a toilet that sat out in the open. Everyone in the cellblock could use the dayroom from morning until lockdown at night.

Out of the dayroom was a corridor that ran between the cells on one side and the guard's catwalk on the other. In the juvenile section, each cell had four bunks: two top and two bottom. Larry and I shared a cell. He had the top bunk on one side and I had the bottom bunk on the other. Being able to move between the dayroom and your cell left lots of room for entertainment with the other inmates. Most of the guys in the pod had messed up at one of the juvenile facilities in Buena Vista, Golden, or at the local Zeb Pike Center. We had much in common.

Larry was content to just read the paper and watch TV, day in and day out. But this was more than I could bear. And so it was up to me to make my own fun.

It was a normal evening in the county jail with everyone on lockdown. Earlier in the day, I had kept my scam going on the white boys. This was the fourth day in a row I had bullied them out of their breakfast, kept them from watching what they wanted to on TV, prevented them from making phone calls, snatched their newspapers and physically blocked their path to the shower. During this time, they had also graciously supplied me with all the cigarettes I could smoke.

These were supposed to be the tough guys of the juvies. One had murdered his parents and the other three were just plain bad. But truthfully, after this many days the game was just a little too easy. There was no challenge left in it.

So when I got wind that the four of them were going to try to persuade me to leave them alone, I went immediately to check on my newest weapon. Yeah, it was there where I had left it, under my mattress. I chuckled to myself at my own genius. Who else but me would have thought to load the toe of a sock completely full of broken pieces of that hard lye soap?

I sat with my back to the bars of my cell and twirled the end of the sock to make it rope-like. Once more I checked to make sure I wasn't being noticed, then I tied the end in a knot and shoved the whole thing down my pants.

No doubt about it, it was an excellent weapon! No lame TV for me. I was ready for some real fun!

By that afternoon, the rumor began to prove itself true. The four white boys knew they'd have one chance and one chance only to take me out. So they came all together to take their best shot.

I was in the dayroom when they rushed me all at once, but before they could come within reach, I pulled out the sock and just began swinging like I was an expert in the martial art of sock defense. I could feel the jolt when that tightly compacted knobby of soap cracked the first guy right on the ear and the second in the nose.

I knew it had to feel like a billy club.

The fact that I had been prepared for their unified attack seemed to put them into shock just long enough for me to maintain the upper hand. I grabbed the third guy and shoved him against the wall, cracking his head repeatedly against the cinder blocks. When his knees buckled, I turned my attention to the fourth kid.

I heard the familiar sound of the door opening and the metallic ringing of the guard's boots on the catwalk. They could see us perfectly through the bars, which separated the catwalk from the cells and dayroom. I had my victim in a headlock and was punching him in the face. The other three were regrouping for another assault. I glanced over long enough to see the guards holding the tear gas canisters.

"Freeze, you MFs, or we'll gas you." The four honkies froze where they were.

"Now, get your asses in your cells." The white boys were eager to get to the protection of their cells, so they went quickly, no questions asked. It's always better to get locked down than beat down.

I knew that if they used the tear gas, it would hit the innocent as well as me, so the chances of them really discharging it were pretty slim. I used this knowledge to bluff the guards. When I finally decided to, I went to my cell.

Eventually, everyone in the block wound up on lockdown.

In the morning after the fight with the white boys, I was awakened by the familiar sound of the cellblock door opening. This time, before I could collect my thoughts, a guard stood outside my cell, "Lee, bag 'em baggies."

He turned and left and my only thought was, "I'm going home." They didn't come and tell you to get your stuff together unless you were going home, did they?

But when the guard returned, he shackled me and pushed me out in front of him. Silently, he led me out into the corridor and then just a short distance to the cellblock next door to the juvies.

So they were bumping me up a notch. Getting me away from all those little kids I was corrupting. I knew their objective was not only to quiet down the juvenile cellblock, but to put me where I'd be taught a lesson. In with the adults.

It was interesting. This new place was like a zoo. Only in this zoo, the animals were staring at me. It didn't take me long to figure it out, though. I was the boy with the rep. The one that was in charge next door. I thought, "I'm a celebrity."

This was good. This was very good.

I wound up spending only a few days in that block, but during that time I had me some fun. One of the brothers took the time to teach me how to play chess and after just two days of practice, I was beating everyone in the cellblock.

We were having a grand time. We'd challenge each other and every so often they'd enroll a new con I hadn't played before. The other guys would try to set him up to lose whatever he had to lose, playing me in chess.

In the end it didn't take the guards long to realize that there were only three things I was being taught in the zoo:

How to play chess.

That chess was a good skill to have for survival.

That I was able to be a master teacher.

"Lee, come on. Bag 'em baggies."

"Where am I going now, pig?"

"A place where you aren't so tough. That's where." We walked clear around to the other side of the compound and the guard slid the extra-large jail door open.

I said, "Man, it's dark in here."

But before I could even finish the sentence, the guard pushed me inside and began to slide the door shut. He announced, "Fresh meat!" Then turned to me and said, "Have fun, Lee." Laughing, he left.

I shivered. This block really wasn't any colder than the others, just the smallness and the darkness made it seem so. The dayroom itself was only about 12' x 12' and instead of three big steel tables there was only one small one. And even though I didn't watch it much, I did wonder where the TV was.

But more impressive than the smothering, dim coldness of the place was the spirit of oppression and hardness that filled the air. I felt it in the tightness in my chest and I knew the guard was right. This place was at least as tough as me. The place was completely no-nonsense. No one came out to see who the new guy was. I was in with a bunch of murderers. Cold, hard murderers, every last one of them.

TEN

My entire body was on full alert as I moved down the corridor. Every movement of my eyes, every twitch of my muscles was no doubt being evaluated, even though I saw no one. I maintained my Oscar-winning, noncommittal stroll as I passed the first cell. It was empty, but I knew better than to stop. It was too close to the guards to take up residence there. It was a cell for scary folk. The second cell was empty also, but likewise, it was too close to the front.

The third cell had someone's stuff in it, but no one was there. My mind continued to race as I struggled to retain control of every detail of my movement. I imagined all the convicts laying in wait in the fourth cell. Waiting to kill me.

In fact, cell number four was not empty, but instead of a desperate ring of conspirators, there was one man, Ray, who resembled someone I knew. I thought for a moment. Joe Frazier! Ray looked like Joe Frazier, except for the eyes. In them was the flitting, unsteady gaze of a frightened animal, or perhaps a young boy lost and alone. But in total, the impression I had of him was that of a friendly gorilla. Built low to the ground, huge biceps protruding through his sleeves, his other muscles straining the very fabric of his clothing, and a face that was leathery and plastic. All the marks of a hard life.

"How you doing, little brother?" His voice was deep and kindly.

With some reserve I answered, "I'm doing fine."

"Why they got you in here?" he asked seriously.

"For fighting. They moved me out of juvie to the adult cellblock for fighting. And from there they brought me here. So for fighting, I guess."

Just then an Indian man stepped from the last cell into the run. His hair was long, thick, black and parted down the middle. He was old, but you couldn't tell how old. He looked both thirty and seventy at the same time. He said, "They don't put you in *here* for fighting. This block is reserved for killers."

I squinted my eyes and shot back, "These pigs ain't gonna put a murder case on me."

The Indian shrugged and returned to his cell. I dismissed the whole conversation and turned back to Ray. "What about the guy in cell number three?"

"He's in court in some other county. I guess he'll be done in a couple of days."

I dropped all my stuff on the floor of cell number three and gathered up all that belonged to the other man. I took it over to cell number one and left it there. I wasn't going to share a cell, and I wasn't going to bunk in no cell for wimps and such like.

"Little brother, never mess with another man's stuff unless you're ready to die." The Indian had returned in time to watch me move things around. I knew his counsel was kindly but I hadn't asked for it.

"Thanks, man," I said. "But I'm prepared to fight for mine." That's all we said. He left and I lay down and fell asleep.

Shortly, I was awakened by a guard's voice. "Lee! Lee! Hey, Lee, you alive in there? If you are, front and center."

I got up and splashed some water on my face, trying to get my bearings. I walked out into the dayroom. Ray and the Indian, Bobby Malone, were sitting at the table, seeing without watching.

The guard pushed some papers through the feeding slot in the door. I heard him say, "Well, you finally made it." Then the feeding slot door slammed shut.

I studied the papers. Hocking had died. Now I was charged with first-degree murder. Bobby Malone leaned back in his chair and finished rolling his cigarette. "I told you they don't put you in here for fighting."

He was right. I was in a place with a bunch of murderers. Cold, hard murderers every one, including me.

ELEVEN

The man whose cell I took never returned, so I didn't have to fight him for it. And eventually, I found out that Ray was a four-time loser, all murders. He had killed his wife, his girl-friend, and three men all at different times. He looked like a gorilla, as I said, but it was more than that. In every way he was like an animal from the bush, now confined. He was filled with hurt and confusion. He told all kinds of stories about his family and about his being a professional weightlifter, but he never spoke of jail. That reality was just too hard, I guess.

On the other hand, Bobby, who turned out to be both black and Indian, was a five-time loser, three of them murders. It was mostly him who took me under his wing and taught me how to cope, how to survive doing time. But even with his help, without the diversions of juvie or the camaraderie of the adult block, the time was *too* hard. And the truth was, I knew I had nowhere else to go from here except the hole. So I decided to set my hopes on getting out.

With the charge against me changed to first-degree murder, my bond went up to $25,000. Mom and Daddy mortgaged the house to raise it, and finally I was released pending trial. My arrest had brought them back together.

Oh, what a happy day! To breathe fresh air and see the sky… it was wonderful to be free!

Larry was out on bond, too, so we took up where we left off, hanging out and chasing skirts. After about three days of freedom, we wound up over at a nondescript house on the north side of town, not too far from where the murder took place, with a whole roomful of beauties. I could feel myself get excited as I watched them move and talk and flirt. They were just beautiful! But in the end, my heart wasn't in it. My mind was still on the cellblock and the counsel of

Bobby Malone and the idea of the hole being close enough to touch. So about 3:00 in the afternoon, I decided to leave. As I went out the door, I glanced back and saw Larry walking a girl down the hall while he was unzipping his fly. I just turned around again, shook my head, and went downtown to the movies.

Hit Man was playing with Bernie Casey. It was a black exploitation kind of movie that everyone was going to see, so I met up with a few guys from the streets on the way in and we sat down together.

It looked to be a quiet evening when about a quarter of the way through the show, I saw one of my girlfriends, Rachel, come strolling in on the arm of some strange guy. She was walking with a twist in her hips and was being all coy and playful. For the second time that day, I got hard. This time my heart got hard with rage.

I waited until they sat down together all cozy and sickening. Then I came up behind her and snatched her hair. Her head snapped back and her chin pointed toward the ceiling.

"Get up, you whore."

She was in shock, but she did what I said. She must have thought I was still in jail. I pulled her around to the side, so I could face the punk who had brought her in.

"You want some of me?" I hissed at him. He and his disappearing cool were still sitting in the seat. He couldn't even form any words in his weasel mouth, so I turned around and dragged Rachel down the theater aisle by her hair.

Outside, I let go of her hair and pushed her along in front of me. "Where's your car, you whore? Take me to your car." She never said anything. She just walked along trying to stay in front of my shoves. Eventually, we got to her car and I made her drive over to the Taco Bell a few blocks away. When we stopped, I slapped her across the face and at the same time shoved her against the driver's side door. I grabbed her throat and cracked her head against the window again and again and again. In the end, I just remember beating the hell out of her for pulling that mess on me.

She stayed conscious the whole time, though, so when I chose to stop hitting her, I made her drive me over to another girl's apartment.

I was going to make her wait while I spent time with the other girl, but I changed my mind. Rachel left and I stayed and just talked to Elaine for about an hour. All my rage was spent. I just walked home after that.

I opened the door to Mom's house and plopped down on the sofa. I was exhausted. That slut had taken everything out of me. I had put my feet up and was just starting to relax when my mom came to the door of the den and said, "Promise Yul, whatever you did, just tell the truth."

My adrenaline began to pump and for a minute I thought of running out the back door. But then I couldn't think of anything I had done that I could be arrested for. Sure, I thought, I had beaten up Rachel, but not *that* bad. I came into the front room and sure enough, there stood the pigs.

"You're under arrest on the charge of rape," one of them said, grabbing my arm.

"Rape? You got to be kidding."

My mom hung her head, "Promise Yul, rape? Boy, have you gone crazy? You better just tell the truth."

Mom just stood there watching and shaking her head as the police loaded me into the back of the police car, again. My bond was immediately revoked and of course, there was no chance of my getting another.

Only this time, I was innocent.

I never really found out the details of what happened after I left that nondescript house, leaving Larry and all those girls behind. But at the hearing on the rape charge, the girl on the witness stand was asked if her attacker was in the room. She said, "Yes."

Then she pointed to Larry and said, "Yes, that's Promise Lee right there." After that the case was dismissed for insufficient evidence.

I think what had happened at the house that day was that Larry had told the girl he was me. He had given her my name before everything went bad. But at the hearing it also came out that the girl, who was white, was pregnant by a black man before any of this happened and that she had just recently been released from the state mental institution.

But regardless of what really happened to the girl that day, both Larry's and my bonds were revoked. I was put back in the murderer cellblock and Larry went back to juvie. We both awaited trial on the Hocking thing.

In the end, Larry and Darrell pled guilty to armed robbery. This meant that if I went to trial, my charge would automatically stick at first-degree murder with no chance of reduction of manslaughter or second-degree murder. If found guilty, I would face the death penalty or life in prison.

I knew I didn't want life or death. So, on a plea bargain, just weeks before I turned sixteen, I pled guilty to second-degree murder, never had a trial, and was sentenced to ten to twelve years in the Colorado State Penitentiary.

TWELVE

The years had worn the paint off the old chest that stood in the corner of the room I shared with my three brothers. I jerked the single left-sided handle on the top drawer until it came open. Now to find the clean shirt that would pass Mom's inspection and grant me passage outdoors. But my hand stopped short when I saw the rat's scaly tail and yellow teeth. Its issue suckled in the manner to which they were born: consuming their very source of life. A lone flea leapt onto my neatly folded shorts.

Startled and repulsed, I closed the drawer.

Now, years later, I saw a second rat that was as vile as the first. This time it came looking for the bologna sandwich that was still waiting to be eaten, still wrapped in brown paper from the prison's kitchen. It moved in the dim light of lockdown, hoping to pass unnoticed. This time I didn't leave a way of escape. I threw my boot toward the rustling. By the sharp, abruptly ended squeal I knew I could safely return to my thoughts.

Perhaps I should be thinking about all the things that were now dead to me. My leisure, my freedom, my childhood. I should be thinking about how many sleepless nights my mother would have. How Mom and Daddy's car was blown up after my conviction. How it is for my brothers and sister having a brother in the penitentiary, a brother who is a murderer. Yet, somehow at fifteen, the bars, the bunk, the cell already seemed like home. It seemed the natural place to be. All the rest was behind.

This night, my first night, was filled with knowledge: that ten years was a long time; that I would have to read and educate myself; that I would have to become a man; that I would have to fight; that I would have to pray. Knowledge that I would have to kill again. Just a few days ago, I had been lying in my bunk at the county jail awaiting the end of my court hearing, the verdict, and the outcome for my life. I was on the bottom bunk on one side and Larry was on the top bunk on the other side in the four-bed holding cell.

My mind was drifting and the whole cellblock was pretty quiet. Suddenly, in my mind, I heard my name being called. Three times I heard the voice call. Then I heard it in my ear: "Promise, Promise, Promise."

I knew I wasn't asleep, so I couldn't be dreaming but I also couldn't figure out where the voice was coming from. I just heard it.

It frightened me. Not the voice. But the mystery of it. I felt like I was going crazy. I had lost control of me and all that was around me. I said to Larry, "Hey, man, did you hear that?"

"What?"

"That voice? I heard a voice calling my name. You didn't hear that?"

"Naw, man. You trippin'."

I laid there a few moments and then said, "Larry, I think I'm going crazy. I think I'm losing my mind, man. I'm hearing voices."

The only thing that kept me from losing my sanity was what he said back. "Look, man. You can't flip out. If you do, what's gonna happen to me?"

Everyone had thought that Larry had been leading me around because he was older. But I knew then, deep inside, that I was going to have to take care of this boy. I was the thinker and the brawler. Larry was the accessory and a good manipulator, too. But what he said pulled me through. He was depending on me.

So I laid there for a while longer and finally went to sleep.

I hadn't realized the voice in my ear was God.

Two days later, I found myself standing before the judge in the dull brown court room. I watched his face twitch as he pronounced the words.

"Promise Lee, I hereby sentence you to a minimum of ten years and maximum of twelve years in the Colorado State Penitentiary."

Rage flooded my soul. Justice had not been done. My face flushed hot and my heart pounded. Justice had not been rendered. In a similar case in Denver, a white boy a year older than me had shot and killed someone, but his parents had money for good defense attorneys and he'd gotten off with less than a year in the boy's reformatory.

My hands were cuffed. The sheriff marched us back to the holding cell. My rage submerged itself as I sat there and waited. I sat there with my head down, saying, "That's a lot of time." I sat there, saying, "I'm glad this thing is over with." I sat there submerging my rage. I sat there.

A few days later, the deputies finally came to transport us to the penitentiary. Handcuffed and shackled, they loaded us into a van. A paper bag containing all our worldly possessions was thrown in after us onto the floor. Larry fidgeted the whole way. But to me, after nearly six months in the county jail without seeing any daylight, the sun just felt too nice. I sat there like a cat, absorbing the sunlight. Closing my eyes in drowsy warmth, as the sun baked the van window. There was no cold-radiating cement, no steel bars. I could barely concentrate on the beautiful scenery as we traveled between Colorado Springs and Cañon City. I just enjoyed the humming of the motor and the beauty of a March afternoon.

I enjoyed it, that is, until we were about a mile from the Pen. That was when I smelled that smell, that smell that turned my stomach. It was there in my memory, somewhere. I could feel it on the edge of my consciousness. I closed my eyes to capture the memory. To my surprise, it was the nursing home where my mom used to work—doing slave labor—cleaning up after old sick white folks. Oh yeah. That was the smell. Putrid death. The smell grew stronger the closer we got to the building.

Even after we entered, we were not allowed to be unshackled. It was only when we had gone inside the bars that they removed the chains. I felt like a dog, off the leash, but still inside the kennel. Inside the Fish Tank.

I suppose I should have seen it coming, but I didn't. The first part of my punishment—a paper raping.

Name:

Date of Birth:

List of personal possessions:

I agree not to perform acts of sodomy and understand that they are a crime, punishable by the state of Colorado.

_____

Signature

Date

   Probing, personal questions as unwelcome as the guard's gloved hand that waited just around the corner. They required answers to topics they shouldn't have any authority over. If you refused to answer them, you would be locked up in the hole until you did. Some guys pretended that they couldn't read, so the questions were read to them. If you absolutely refused to submit to this paper rape, you were shipped to the state hospital in Pueblo. Some of those guys became part of an experiment with a new drug called Thorazine that left them not caring about anything.

   While I was enduring my paper raping, a Mexican guy walked down the stairs bouncing a black rubber ball. I figured he was either a trustee or a snitch, one of the two. He had a red bandana on his head and another on his arm. He kept bouncing that handball real hard against the steel step and catching it with a snap. At one point he caught it and held it for a moment. This was the break my partner was looking for. Larry said, "Hey, man, do we get to play ball in here?"

   By the tone of his voice, I could tell that he was afraid and trying to make friends. The Mexican bounced the ball real hard, caught it and said, "Yeah, you get to play all kinds of ball here." Then he grabbed his nuts. I looked him right dead in the eye and we stared at each other for about twenty seconds. Then he left. He disappeared up the steps.

I'd run into him again. My instinct told me it wouldn't be nice. I finished my paperwork and got my number, 42885. It fit me. It fit me like my green shirt and pants and my Brogan shoes with the "V" cut in the heel... high tops. All of it fit me to a T. Five feet, six inches and 145 pounds of muscle. It all fit just right. I felt and looked like a seasoned convict.

They put me on the third tier and Larry on the first. When I went up, everything was silent. Everything was locked down.

It was about 5:00 p.m. We had arrived too late for supper. That's why they gave me that bologna. I went in my cell with my blanket and all that stuff and the door closed electronically behind me. I laid down on my bunk.

After a while I heard someone say, "Promise Lee, is that you?"

I got up and went to the cell bars and said, "Yeah."

Animal in a cage,
Boy full of rage,
Pacing the floor
No where to go,
Even if they crack the door.

Locked up? Locked down?
Confined,
Everything except my mind.

Doin Time.

Promise Lee, 1974

THIRTEEN

The panorama of a Japanese cityscape moved before my eyes. You could see a long way from the roof of our apartment building, where lots of other American GIs lived. I stood with my father and his friends, the men. I was five. I don't know what they were talking about, but I felt special just to be there with the men. Just then Daddy picked me up to get a better view. It was wonderful to be held close, up high, and to be there in the company of men. I don't know what happened then. I mean, I don't know why he did it. But suddenly, he held me over the edge of the building. This is the picture I remember better. What the city looked like from the top, forty stories up. My stomach churned as the air rushed past my face. I had to pee. The street and cars below seemed to rush toward my eyes, and while my lunch seemed to be moving toward my mouth, my stomach dropped toward my feet. My eyes burned. I wouldn't cry. This is what I remember better. Not what it is to feel like a man, but what it is to be a helpless boy. To this day, I have a certain phobia of heights.

My leg was securely wrapped around a pole as I leaned nervously over the guardrail, surveying four stories of cells and what seemed like thousands of stories of convicts. My heart jumped when two inmates brushed past me. I just couldn't get over this height thing. I decided to ease away from the rail. It was just as well. Just then the guard came to take me down to testing.

It was part of the raping that I had naively thought had ended two days earlier when we arrived. Now, though, instead of a paper raping, I would have to endure a mind raping. They had warned me that Levy, the psychologist, would do anything to get a reaction: pull a gun or knife on you, maybe even try to hit you. I knew they'd do anything to make you expose your hand. Then they would know how to play you, how to strip you of your power, and then, when you're naked, how to snatch your manhood from you. Everyone knows that rape isn't only about sex. It's about draining a person's power out of them. I wished I could drain the power out of Dr. Joyce Gamewell and the other psychobabble broads who thought they could evaluate my psychological condition.

It was a long walk to the testing lab. For a while I tried to count the cinder blocks as we walked past... twenty-seven... twenty-eight. It was like being a kid and trying to count the cars while you were stopped at the railroad crossing. They went by too fast to really count, but it kept your mind off how long it was taking.

Outside the testing lab there were already a lot of numbers waiting. We were all scheduled for 1:00 p.m. I sat on a wooden bench outside the door for a long time. This was part of the game: To make you so frustrated, you would give them what they wanted.

Slowly, the door to the room opened. There were lots of guards inside, and desks. Lots of desks. Otherwise, it was just as plain as the cinder-block halls.

"Form a single row along the back, convicts," a guard growled.

Then, another guard started calling out numbers and pointing to assigned seats with papers already on them. I watched as the numbers were called, but I didn't recognize anybody.

Third row, second from the front. It was as good a seat as any to get raped from. I turned the paper over.

QUESTION 1: Do you hear bells?

QUESTION 2: Do you love your mother?

QUESTION 3: If you were driving and there was something in the road would you:

    A. Go around it

    B. Go over it

QUESTION 4: Do you hear voices?

QUESTION 5: Do you hate your mother?

Questions? Questions! Questions. Sometimes you could tell how to answer, sometimes you couldn't. It reminded me of those tests in second and third grade when they asked how many saucers did I see, but all I saw were little plates. And when I asked my teachers the questions, like, why doesn't anyone in these books look like me? And why is Santa Claus white? Asking such questions, and simultaneously wanting to satisfy my appetite for knowing, regularly got me in trouble. I was labeled as a smart alec.

Questions.

Where was that Levy guy? Was he going to face me? Go one on one? Man to man?

He never did show up.

Rape? Rape! Rape.

Out in the yard the sun was shining. It felt good to breathe real air and see the sky.

I listened to the gossip in the yard. A couple of faggots had just come through a day or so ago. Tension was high. It seemed like every time one would come in, there was a fight to see whose property they would turn out to be. So anything might happen. I checked to make sure the magazines I had sewn into the lining of my jacket were still in place. They might not stop a shank completely, but I'd probably live to kill the guy who'd try to stick me.

I enjoyed real fights, but here they needed to call them something else. Win or lose, it was never over—unless, of course, you were the dead one. Mostly, it was the strong pitted against the weak. One guy got whipped to death... *Maybe in awhile I will get a faggot and make him wash my clothes. I like that lye soap. It takes all the oiliness right out of your skin.*

"Four-two-eight-eight-five, in here... Now!"

I entered the office and the guard closed the door behind me. It had taken more than a week, but now I finally got to meet him—the infamous Dr. Levy. Seeing him, I felt a little more relaxed.

Behind the desk was a short, pudgy man, gray all over. His coat was gray. His white shirt was gray. His hair was gray. His skin was gray. Even his teeth were gray. Dried snot was stuck to the hairs growing out of his nose and matted to his mustache. I also noticed he bit his fingernails to the nub.

So this was the cracker who was going to make me give it up! I could take this guy out without even touching him. I could make him wet his pants just by looking at him. If I wanted to, I could make him my girlfriend. He was a cinder block, not worth counting.

All I have to do is let this guy know not to mess with me. Then we'll see whose prisoner's whose.

"Convict, tell me about your parents." A New York accent.

"What's to tell?"

"Are they from Colorado?"

"Nope."

Levy sprang up onto the top of his desk and waved his arms around like he thought he knew karate or something. So this is what they meant when they said he'd do anything. What a cat! I held my eyes steady. Didn't open 'em wide. Didn't squint. Didn't blink. Didn't smile. Didn't frown. Didn't flinch.

"Do you have brothers and sisters, Convict?" he screamed, hovering over me from the top of the desk.

"Yep. You got all that on your paper, though, Shrink."

His gray eyes narrowed. He jumped down from his desk to a spot just inches from my chair. He leaned his dingy face forward and I could smell his gray breath. I stared into his colorless eyes.

"Maybe you'd feel more comfortable if we didn't talk about real people. Do you ever have dreams?"

"Hee hee. Yeah. My favorite ones are wet ones. Come to think of it, I dreamed about you just last night."

"Okay, you want to be smart. Let's start with your test results."

My eyes were still locked on his. I hadn't blinked.

Animal in a cage... Boy full of rage... Never, never break the gaze!

FOURTEEN

I sit in the middle of an empty room. I am naked. I am cold. I can scarcely move.

Breathe, NOW, breathe!

I am aware that I am getting smaller. I am aware that the room is getting larger.

All I hear is my heart. thumpTHUMP. thumpTHUMP. thumpTHUMP. thumpTHUMP. thumpTHUMP.

I am an ant in a huge empty building. I run and run and run. The smaller I get, the more I run.

Where am I now? I'm getting smaller. I can't see myself. Where am I?

Where am I?

Everything is in slow motion. I struggle and strain. I get nowhere.

I've got... to move... I've got... to lift... my foot... I've got... to run....

I am helpless. I am small. It is hopeless. I cannot escape.

UUUUGH!

Awake. The sound of my gasp is deafening. I am dripping with sweat and freezing cold. It has been years since I dreamed that dream.

Where's a shrink when you need him? Where is that gray boy?

After sixty days of the system's "help," my resistance and hostility were undaunted and so I was designated for maximum security. I guess they thought I was high risk.

I was glad.

I wanted to do my time and get out. I didn't want to mess around with "rewards" and "consequences" and moving up levels and all that kindergarten junk. If I had to kill my number, I'd rather do it in maximum security.

Still, Levy was the only man who could walk all through the Pen, behind the walls and everywhere, without a guard escort. Everyone knew he was your ticket out. If Levy said, "Let him go," you were out. So there wasn't no one going to kill him.

I eventually answered all his questions. But he never knew that.

The year I first dreamed that dream about getting smaller and not escaping was the same year I went up on the roof in Japan with my dad. It was the same year I started kindergarten and began going to the stairwell with Brigade. It was also the year my brother Charmas was born. I was named after my father, who was born at the same time his Indian grandfather was dying. My father was the promise of life renewing itself, and I was his Promise. My brother Thomas was named Thomas just because my mom liked the name. But when her third son was born, a Japanese lady who saw him remarked that he was "just charming." So Charmas became his name and his trademark.

Eat, sleep, exercise. Eat, sleep, exercise. The routine of the Fish Tank was wearing on me. Nixon was leaving office after the Watergate scandal. Patty Hearst had been kidnapped, and the 55-mile speed limit had been enacted all over the country, but none of that affected us.

I looked forward to the diversion that Saturdays would bring. We were allowed contact visits. Mom and Daddy would be coming, bringing someone with no panties on. Mom was determined I wouldn't be turned out. There in the sunlight of the yard, I let my mind wander, thinking about my girls who had come to visit. Alicia had been here. Then Renata. It had gotten so that every Saturday morning I'd wake up with a hard on.

One visiting room was shared by both the Fish Tank and maximum. They had cameras, but the cameras couldn't watch everyone all the time. So every week, after a little visit with my folks, my girl would come and sit on my lap without her panties. It was real easy to avoid being on camera. And with all that waiting between Saturdays, it would be real rewarding.

Yes, for a while the Pen seemed better than any home I'd had. Three hots and a cot and a girl every week. But after a while, seeing folks from home made the time between Saturdays just too hard to do. I would be looking forward to it instead of watching my back. It put your mind back on the streets. It put your mind back home. And this was a war zone. So I took all the visitors off my list. And for a time, I just let the sunshine in the yard warm me instead.

The yard was alive, like a beehive. The confines of unlimited activity. Swarms of convicts hovered around the weights, watching brothers pump iron. Others darted back and forth in the rhythm of a handball game, just as a bee moves in and out of an open blossom. Still others worked together to defeat a rival basketball team, defending their hoop as if it were a queen. I joined the few who traveled the periphery, monitoring all the activity. All of us were armed. All of us had shanks.

I looked up and saw Mississippi Petee coming toward me. He was about fifty and a country bumpkin and wannabe pimp who pretended he was involved in big things outside. In the Pen you always knew who was arriving and what their charge was. Petee's charge was so minor, we didn't even hear about it. His fat face was expressionless as he approached. When he stopped in front of me, though, and showed me all the gold in his mouth, I knew it could mean only one thing—he wanted me to write another letter back home, a letter to one of the girls he was pimping.

"Hey, Li'l Bro. How sharp do you think you are?" he asked.

I didn't answer him right away. I just looked at him thinking that maybe he couldn't write and wondering whether this was the reason he always asked *me* to put his thoughts on paper. So before I could answer him about being sharp, he said, "I'll give you the address of this woman right now if you think you can catch her."

I looked down at the picture he was holding. Two women beamed from the photograph. One was white and one was black.

"The black one's my woman," he announced, "but this here

white woman is Valerie and if you think you can catch her, I'll give you the address."

I knew Petee was trying to bring things right. He didn't want to ask me to write a letter for him again without "paying" for my services. So I said I'd take the address partly to see if I could get the woman, but mostly so I could help out old Petee.

Back in my cell we sat down together to write his letter. He dictated, I wrote just what he told me. He inquired about the other girls he was pimping, how business was going, and about the other cats on the street. No big news to give or receive, just a letter home.

After he left, I wrote to the address he'd used as payment. It was the first of many letters I wrote to Valerie.

"Mail call!"

The guard carelessly tossed an envelope through the bars of my cell. The stamp had been removed to prevent any LSD from being sealed behind it.

Just the smell of the envelope was a comfort. It was from Valerie. The letter inside smelled just as good, but I struggled to read it.

In addition to her bad handwriting, she wrote in broken English. She was German and twenty-nine years old. I was sixteen. She worked at the Denver Airport. She asked me to put her on my visitor list. I did.

She came the next weekend and lots of weekends after that, even after they stopped the contact visits. She and her letters were a comfort. It wasn't like seeing someone from home to stir up all that emotion, the kind that can get you killed.

But still, she was a live person, someone to train your thoughts on. I could depend on her to write and visit. She wasn't a piece of home, but she was a friend.

The light outside my cell cast vertical shadows across my bunk. Bars beyond bars. The chatter from the other inmates had slowly died down. Every cell was filled with silence, but not peace.

My dream from that one night was still haunting me and I strained to remember more of that time in Japan. I closed my eyes.

In a small place I could remember another friend. A Japanese boy. A friend other than Brigade. We were about six years old and used to go to the park together and gather up all the kumquats that had fallen on the ground. We would run and chase each other and have contests. Then we would sit down together and eat all those kumquats. He didn't know English and I didn't know Japanese, but we always had the grandest times. We didn't see color or race then. For a long time I kept a picture of him. I had liked to look at it, even after we moved back to the states. It seemed like it had been a long time ago, but it still made me feel happy just to see his face.

I still can't remember his name. But what I do remember better of that time in Japan is that Brigade came and got me nearly every day, and whether awake or asleep, my dream rarely left me. I don't need a picture to see her face nor have my eyes closed to see that dream.

FIFTEEN

Waiting. Waiting. I'd been in Cañon City for three days. I stood behind the bars of my 6' x 8' cell waiting for the guards to crack my door. Below me, tiers one through three had been released to go to chow. The population looked like ants in an ant farm, swarming through little tunnels between panes of glass as if they had somewhere to go. Some traveled in single-file lines; others stood waiting outside their cells. Workers moved back and forth between unidentifiable destinations.

I could see the movement of their minds, even in those who stood still. Indeed, I had never seen so many men in uniform in one place at one time. They seemed like zombies from the *Twilight Zone*. Under the influence of the mind-controlling, mad scientist, they were marching to their destinies… or in this case, the chow hall.

"Fourth tier!" the guard yelled.

Chi-CHANK. Clank. My door slid open: metal on metal. Quickly, I stepped out onto the runway that stretched between the cell doors and the tier railing.

I looked left. I looked right. Everything seemed cool, so I stepped forward into line. When I did, my stomach turned over.

Man! Why did they put me so high up? Only a puny iron railing stood between me and the floor four stories straight down. It reminded me of being in Japan with my dad and suddenly I felt pissed off.

My herd of cattle moved obediently down the line and onto the stairs, which led to the dining hall. I saw Larry at the bottom.

"Hey, man, how's it on first tier?" I asked.

He mumbled something I couldn't understand. Larry was hitting the downers. I didn't really say much more.

In the chow line I picked up my steel tray. The smooth metal was cold to the touch and it turned anything they served on it cold, too.

I couldn't bear the sucking sound the slop made when it plopped off the spoon or the look of it splattering onto the tray. Gray gruel on a gray tray on a gray day. I looked away.

I instantly made eye contact with a Mexican at the end of the line. It was the same snitch, or whatever, who had been there when Larry and I first arrived a few days ago. He still wore his red bandana.

Knowing who he was, I wasn't about to break the gaze. I didn't want to let him think I was weak. Even still, he winked at me and this time instead of just grabbing his privates, he rubbed his palm over his crotch in a real nasty fashion.

I knew that one come-on was bad enough, but now I had to put an end to this bull before I found myself being somebody's girl. So, I held my eyes steady and continued down the line, just like nothing happened. But the reality is, as I was running my tray along the cafeteria rail, I was mustering up all the strength I had. The muscles in my chest twitched and I flexed my biceps to pump them up. When I got to the end of the counter, I eased over like I was just moving out of line. With a snap I brought the edge of the tray up with all the force I had, using it to smash the Mexican's nose up and back into his head. Instantly blood spurted everywhere, giving me the chance to pound his face.

I went to work on him, feeling the soft tissue of his face give way under my fists and the sticky dampness of blood oozing over my knuckles.

I started to lift him up by his collar to give me a better punching angle, when I noticed a rifle trained directly on me. I looked around a full 360 degrees and counted half a dozen guards similarly poised, ready to blow my head off.

Slowly I eased the Mexican back to the floor and looked at my tray. I'll be damned if that Mexican's face hadn't bent the hell out of it. Ever so smoothly, I raised my hands over my head.

What a difference from county jail. Just because of that little fight, armed guards had been called out. All five hundred inmates missed breakfast and the entire cell house went on lockdown for the rest of the day. I guess everyone now knew I had arrived.

The whole time they were scooping the Mexican up off the floor to take him to the infirmary, he was cursing and screaming and swearing his revenge on me, "I'm gonna kill you, nigger."

He was hurting, that's for sure. But as for me, I felt good.

SIXTEEN

I was sixty-five days in the Fish Tank while the Colorado State Penitentiary diagnosed me. Here I was tested, prodded, poked, and analyzed. They wanted to find out if I was a good prisoner or a bad one. A convict who would make trouble or a convict who marched by their drumbeat. Of course, they tried to brainwash me into being good. In the end, though, it didn't really matter who you were. It only mattered who you made people *think* you were. That's what got you places.

Before I was sentenced, my attorney Tom Armour had explained that I was going to hear things in court that might make me mad, but to just keep my cool. He was trying as hard as he could to keep me out of the Pen because I was just a little kid.

But it didn't really matter that I was a little kid and could easily be killed in the Pen. Mr. Armour had to prove to the judge that there were other reasons why I shouldn't go. So, he gathered a bunch of test results. Test results that said I had below average intelligence and could be manipulated. That I was confused about my sexuality and could be turned out. That I needed counseling, not confinement.

I thought about those things in the Fish Tank, especially about what a waste of time all that psychological crap was. I also wrote to Mr. Armour all the time. I felt lucky. He wrote back. Most cats hadn't heard from their attorneys since sentencing. He was working on getting my sentence reduced, but he told me again to keep my cool and count on doing at least two years and concentrate on educating myself. It seemed crazy to me, but he was sure he could get my time shortened. So I did my best to hang on and wait.

I decided to take his advice and made up in my mind that I would read everything I could get my hands on—magazines, newspapers, encyclopedias, even the dictionary. Everything. Everything. Even the Bible.

I had my reservations about reading the Bible because of all the sanctimonious folks I'd been around when I was a kid. Their lives just seemed to be going through the motions. You know, carrying a suitcase with nothing in it. Dressing up on Easter, but functioning as Lucifer the other 364 days of the year.

I just couldn't figure it out. All those black people going to church Sunday after Sunday, talking about how God cared for us and loved us and all the while pointing to Michelangelo's depiction of a white Jesus and white angels and white saints. And how after a while everything I was wondering about right now was going to be all right. Anyone could feel in the air that things were not all right. Racism was everywhere—in the workplace, in the schools, in the parks, in the playground, everywhere. You didn't have to see it. You could feel it. And then the preacher would preach that alcohol and dope were enemies to mankind and later say, "Love your enemy."

It all seemed so confusing. So when I decided to read the Bible, I decided to read it in a different way, like research. Like researching the research.

So I read everything I could get my hands on. And when my girlfriends would write and want to send money, I'd write back and tell them to send me magazine subscriptions. So I read and read and read.

Before I left the Fish Tank, I had asked all the big questions. Who am I? Why am I? Where am I? Am I a political prisoner? Am I even guilty?

Yes. I was and am guilty. Guilty of protecting myself. Guilty of defending myself. Guilty of surviving. Guilty of playing the hand that was dealt to me. Guilty of trying to live the kind of life I'd seen on TV and in magazines, where all the homes are neat, all the families are whole, all the tables are laden with food, and all the jobs earn you a living wage.

Yes, I had come to the conclusion that I was, in fact, guilty of what *they* called *murder* and what I called *self-defense*. But I had made up in my mind that from now on, I'd never be guilty of self-defense again. Never be guilty because I would never be on the defense again. I would always be on the offense. Never again would anyone pose a threat to me. Not physically. Not mentally. Not economically. Not intellectually. Not emotionally. Not politically. And certainly not spiritually.

Reading everything is how I prepared for perpetual offense. I also continued to do the Jack LaLane exercises I'd learned from TV as a kid and to pump iron. I studied martial arts under two mentors. And in the sixty-five days in the Fish Tank, I began my journey as an untouchable convict.

On the other side of the world, Mr. Armour was doing his job and he was right. He got the judge to change my sentence from ten to twelve years to zero to twelve. Having an indeterminate sentence like that made me eligible to be transferred to Buena Vista, a medium-security facility in the mountains.

But instead, both Larry and I were moved to the medium-security facility in Cañon City, just a stone's throw away from Max. This was as I had suspected it might be.

In medium they gave convicts a choice about whether to live in a cell or a dorm-like place. Each had disadvantages. The cells offered less freedom of movement and freedom in general. The dorms, just because of their openness, increased the probability of killing or being killed.

I would never be on the defense again.

I chose the dorm.

April 11, 1975

Promise Lee
Box 1010, Register No. 42885
Cañon City, Colorado 81212

Dear Promise:

I've received your letter and progress reports from your mom, Jackie Williams, and others. I'm not going to write you weekly, but I do want to correspond regularly. In any event, I expect you to write me more often.

Darrell was sentenced this morning to the Colorado State Reformatory for a term not to exceed eight years. The probation officer recommended a penitentiary term, but Gallagher thought Darrell's prior record and somewhat slighter involvement warranted a direct sentence. The whole matter is probably academic since Darrell really has a bad attitude. It will only be a matter of time before he is in trouble again. I don't want you talking "wipe" about him or your sentence. Your conduct can earn you a release earlier than your term. Your sentence can be commuted or you can be placed in the external placement program before the parole eligibility date.

What you need to do now is cooperate with the diagnostic people, which I hear you have done. And don't listen to inmate advice. If you don't blow it yourself, you will be transferred. You still have the right to a 35(a) sentence reduction hearing if you are denied a transfer.

You start thinking long term. I want two hard years of work out of you. Start reading, writing, and planning a legitimate future. Build your body and mind. You have a better attitude than Darrell and can make it.

Keep writing and tell me what you're reading. I'm going to start grading your papers for spelling and grammar on white man's terms.

Respectfully,
Tom W. Armour

TWA/dkd

My body's being held by bricks and bars.
Someone please tell me who's really the cause.
Men, like animals, have the right to survive.
Why have I been penalized for staying alive?

Promise Lee
1975

SEVENTEEN

S ixty-five days after entering the Fish Tank, we left, handcuffed and shackled. They loaded Larry and me into a van and hauled us over to this very different kind of place—to M.S. A guard signed for us like we were packages. With very few words, they shuffled us back behind the bars and began to repeat the paper rap- ing we had received coming into the Fish Tank. I supposed I was get- ting used to it because it didn't bother me as much this time.

Medium Security, or M.S., as we called it, was a very different kind of place from the Fish Tank. We were allowed contact visits again and other small perks. But the biggest difference was that I was given a choice about where I wanted to live: dorm or cell.

Most of the guys in the dorms had big time, like William Garrison, for instance. He had a life sentence like lots of the convicts. But he was different. He had been there for years and had actually been escorted down "the hall of death" several times. Each time, though, he had been given a stay of execution and had been in the news as a result.

Every motionless line in his face warned that he was a no-non- sense kind of a cat. Like his face, his actions were always calm—a little too calm. Calm like smoldering ashes. No flame. No warning of danger. Just soothing warmth that belied a potential inferno. He called me Little Brother.

"Come on, Lee. Let's give you the grand tour of your new home," the guard said, his face twitching, or maybe smirking. I was- n't sure.

We walked down a long, empty corridor that was lined with what I guessed were administrative offices, then through some barred entrances and back into the facility itself, like Jonah entering into the bowels of a big fish, able to run from men, but not from God. The sound of the gates clanking shut was the same no matter where you were, Max, M.S., or the belly of the big fish.

"Now, this here is the dorm," he said flatly, interrupting my thoughts.

I gazed into a long, narrow room with rows of bunks lining the short ends. In between were waist-high dividers. These, too, had beds lined up along either side. In all, I guess there were about thirty beds in this one room.

There were metal lockers like we had had in gym class where you could keep your cigarettes and other stuff you didn't want stolen. A large group bathroom, again, like in the boys' junior high school locker room, was at the far end.

Being in that big room made me a little nervous. If I chose to live here, would I ever sleep? How could anyone sleep in jail without bricks and bars to keep the predators out?

I heard myself tell the guard, "I'll live here."

"Don't want to see the cells, huh?"

"I'll live here," I repeated as much to myself as to him.

"Suit yourself. I'll fill out the papers." He left me unattended and at the mercy of those already in residence.

"Is that you, Promise Lee?" a voice called from behind me. Hesitantly, I turned around. Seeing Bullet Proof, I exhaled in relief, conscious that I was letting my shoulders droop as my breath escaped. I made a mental note not to make an error like that again, a sign of weakness.

"Hey, Bullet Proof. How ya been?"

For a long moment we looked at each other, evaluating whether time had changed anything. Bullet Proof was a guy I had known briefly on the streets. He was from a place called Widefield, just southeast of Colorado Springs. I was a Southsider. We had both been kings of our own domain. We'd had respect. Now we sized each other up to see if it was still due.

In the face, Butch looked like a black Teddy Roosevelt. He got the name Bullet Proof because he'd been shot by the police more than forty times. When he took his shirt off him, it had holes just about everywhere. But he was still alive and had no disabilities. He moved around slow, but then, he always had.

After a long moment, an almost imperceptible nod passed between us. We were cool.

Bullet Proof's number was old. I hadn't realized he'd been down for so long. But I guess it was lucky for me. He got me a bunk near his and as I was still getting settled in, he said, "Look, man," as he pointed to the vacant bed between his and mine, "if you ever need to do somebody, here it is."

Under the mattress laid a self-styled knife, a sword, and a machete just waiting to be employed. I nodded and unrolled my mattress.

After I got my stuff arranged, Butch toured me around. Everyone respected him. He walked that slow, peaceful kind of walk, like a stroll, and said only what needed to be said. As the cons passed us in the corridor, they would pay allegiance to him saying, "Hi, Butch," "Hello, Butch," "What's up, Butch?" His expression never changed. He'd just nod his head in the same almost imperceptible way he'd nodded to me earlier.

It felt good walking along like this. Powerful. Ready for action. Just waiting for my chance to make some sucker respect me. We just kept walking, and when we finished the tour of the cell house and dorm, we walked out to the yard.

The yard at M.S. was bigger than the Fish Tank's, but the activities were just the same—except for the big boxing ring at one end. In a split second I was spellbound.

There, getting ready to box, was a huge, black gorilla-looking guy. He was putting on gloves, getting ready to fight the big young brother already in the ring and smiling like he didn't have good sense. As they squared off, he seemed to prove my hypothesis that he didn't have good sense. The gorilla just stood there with his head out. The young brother punched and punched but accomplished nothing but misses.

Finally, the gorilla said, "I want the worm."

POW! He knocked the young guy out, took off his gloves, woke the young guy up, and said, "See you in a few."

I stood there bewildered. I looked over at Butch's six-foot-four, 260-pound frame and for the first time I saw him smile. "That's Harvey Banks. He's a faggot."

"What? Him?" I replied, startled.

"Man, see how built he is? He used to be a pro boxer, but he ended up in here. But don't be fooled. He likes men. He's going to approach you. Don't entertain him. Be firm and say no. If you show any weakness, he'll ask you every day, all day, and then try to trick you. Just tell him no."

But days passed without hearing anything from Harvey. That wasn't really like him. Usually, he had no mercy on "new fish." I vaguely wondered what was taking him so long and I entertained the thought that he was afraid of me.

Butch was right, though. Eventually, Harvey approached me. One day I met him in passing. "Hey, you want me to bring you some sandwiches from the kitchen?" Harvey worked in the mess hall and was one of the few cons with the ability to get extra food.

"Yeah. When?" I accepted the challenge.

"After dinner come down to my space and get them."

I waited but never went down. After a while Harvey came up to get me instead. I was lying on my bed reading.

"What you doing here, Harvey," Butch asked.

"I come to talk to Little Brother."

"I don't think he wants to talk to you, Harvey."

"Naw, Butch. I *do* want to talk to him."

Then I commanded Harvey, "Bring me my sandwiches before I get mad and you better hurry up." Butch looked at me like I had gone crazy. Then he looked at Harvey.

"Okay," Harvey said. And he smiled that same boxing-ring smile I saw the first time I laid eyes on him. "I'm afraid of people who get mad," he cooed. Then he left. But he didn't return.

"What the hell is wrong with you, boy? Have you lost your mind? That nigger will kill you," Butch nagged.

I didn't answer. I just smiled to myself and went back to reading.

A few days later I ran into Harvey again, but he never said a word to me. It made me wonder what was on his mind. In fact, that whole week Harvey was knocking people out, "taking the worm," but not in the ring.

Toward the end of the week, I ran downstairs to the basement dorm to look at some artwork by a friend of mine. Harvey was the last thing on my mind, so I wasn't strapped. I didn't even have on a coat. The hallway was dark and the whole dorm seemed soundproof. You couldn't hear any of the regular noises. The quiet put me on my guard and as I rounded the corner, there was Harvey. All 250 pounds of him. And there was me. All 145 pounds of me, with no shank and no protection.

His stare was cold and motionless. I knew I was going to have to fight for my life and yet I knew I couldn't begin to whip him. For the first time the thought of dying in the Pen entered my mind. What would the headlines read? KILLED BY A FAGGOT? Of course, my mom wouldn't know. Harvey could easily be mistaken for a football player or even a Mike Tyson.

For the moment, all I knew was that I couldn't shift my gaze, couldn't drop my head. Any flinch would be read as a sign of weakness and that would be the death knell.

"I want the worm. Give me the worm." Harvey's voice droned like it was in slow motion. Suddenly, his hardened face cracked just the faintest hint of a smile and inside a wave of relief ran through me.

His concentration on "the worm" had been broken ever so slightly. I knew I had room to maneuver. He was bluffing me now. Trying to put fear in my heart. The kind of fear that could make me his girlfriend. But he had shown me his hand. He was like a dog, close enough to bite, but choosing to growl instead.

I focused all my concentration on his right eye, staring hard and relentlessly. "You ain't taking anything and I ain't giving you anything. Man, who do you think I am? I ain't a boy. Now move out of my way before you really make me mad."

Then pushing forward, with a tight frown powering my movements and flexed muscles puffing me up like some bizarre desert lizard, I chided, "Harvey, don't make me have to kill you."
Having passed him, I turned around and caught his eye again.

"Hey man, don't you ever try to play me like that again. You almost pissed me off."

I never had any more trouble out of Harvey. But I knew I had made him mad and he'd let me slide. He could have blocked my path or rushed me and then I would have had to go to Plan B. The truth is that Plan A wasn't a plan and I sure didn't have a Plan B. I guess

Plan A was to get my butt out of there as quick as possible and B was before it's too late.

Isn't it something, the way God watches over fools? Man, how God watches over fools. I think that was the second time God spoke to me, but again I didn't hear him.

EIGHTEEN

I realized that M.S. was both a testing ground and a teaching ground, and I would have to pass the test. You see, M.S. was a quiet place. In the seven or so months I spent there, I can hardly remember a shanking or even lockdowns for that matter.

Here the battle was fought on a different plane. A higher plane. The weapons were heads, not hands. Brains, not brawn. Most of the prisoners were competing against the system, not each other. Stamps were more desired than knives. Practically everyone in there knew how to file a writ with the court. And mail call was sacred, invoking a kind of power that was palpable.

I lay on my bunk reading while, with one ear, I listened to the evening chatter that was a part of medium-security prison life. Butch wasn't much of a reader, but always respected me and didn't interfere with mindless conversation when I was trying to concentrate. I appreciated that about him.

That's why he spoke so softly when he had visitors, but it also disturbed me that I couldn't always hear what was going on. It was a matter of protection. So one night when Spoon came down to see Butch, I put my book down and strolled the few paces over to his bed.

"Hey, man, meet Little Brother," Butch nodded toward me. I hated to be referred to as "Little" anything. It was like being a grown man and being called Junior or Sonny. It was demeaning.

"How ya doing," Spoon extended his hand. I nodded and returned the greeting. I had heard of this guy. He was over the Black Studies Program. I'd heard he was deep, but I never took anything for granted.

"So what good is Black Studies when we're all in here and they're all out there?" I asked, testing him.

Spoon's deep, good-natured chuckle preceded his response. "Well now, Little Bro, seems like if you don't know the answer to that, you need some studies."

"Yeah. That'd be good, Promise. Why don't you come on?"

"I…," I started to decline, but Spoon jumped in too quick.

"We're putting a play together now. They're going to let us perform it here and at the women's prison."

That was all either of them needed to say. I was convinced I needed Black Studies based on the sheer lack of in-the-flesh women in my life.

So it was, that my carnal desires opened up perhaps the most spiritual doors in my life—ever. As a natural consequence of the play rehearsals, I began to learn things I had never begun to imagine. I studied Islam. Egyptology. Slavery. The more I learned about myself, the more my feelings were validated—against the Black church of worshipping a white God, against my father for his obsession with the French language and white women. All were validated by what I read and learned.

And my furor swelled whenever I wondered why I had not learned about the contributions and nobility of Black people in school. Had they hidden these facts from me? Intentionally? I felt betrayed, confused, and empowered all at the same time.

I began to listen better and to sharpen my thinking skills. I became more analytical in my approach to problems. I challenged thoughts and ideas, even if I intuitively sensed they were correct. I was confirmed in my belief that the best defense is a potent offense, and so I honed my mind into a weapon capable of killing or giving life at my discretion.

I became one of them. The youngest one of them. And the badge of "Little Brother" I now wore with pride, humble in my understanding that I knew little of what it took to be a man.

Grow up

One day I think I want to grow up.
I want to grow up so I don't hurt anymore.
I want to grow up so I don't hurt anyone anymore.
I want to grow up so I don't hurt alone anymore.
I want to grow up.

Promise Lee, 1976

NINETEEN

S poon was a great inspiration to me. And so it was on one of those M.S. nights that I lay on my bunk and contemplated the truly great men in my life. The ones who had come before Spoon and tried to show me the way.

Role models for me were not athletes because their behavioral success seemed to be something I could easily attain. I knew in third grade I could be a pro football player (running back). I knew in fifth grade I could eventually break Jesse Owens' records. I also knew I could eventually beat anybody in tennis. Role models to me at that time were mostly people I had actual contact with. People who did things that were not based so much upon physical or athletic ability, but instead upon the sacrifice of themselves for others. I was told that Col. Bryant, whose son I grew up with, was an original Harlem Globetrotter. He stood very tall and very wide. His hands were so big and strong looking, it seemed like he could palm two basketballs in one hand. His voice was deep and gravelly and he only talked when he had something to say.

When I was nine or so, I found out the neighborhood boys were on an all-black baseball team and I couldn't wait to join. Mostly, I played in the outfield, although sometimes I substituted other positions. The only position I never played was catcher. I was terrified of getting hit with a bat.

Col. Bryant took us all over the city to play and we were good. He'd come to Fountain Park in his old brown station wagon that was torn up from driving around a bunch of kids and he'd pull out bags of baseball bats, gloves and balls. Then he'd pile all of us in there for games, sometimes making two trips. It's amazing how some of his habits have stuck with me, even to this day. I have coached track and basketball in several schools and ruined a van and a car from hauling kids to and from practices and games. Col. Bryant was a proud man. Not cocky, but proud. He gave of his time. I never heard him curse or get angry at a kid. In my book, the only thing he was guilty of was helping those in need.

Then there was Uncle Bud. He looked like a cowboy, if you just looked at his legs. In junior high, kids used to play games, running down the halls and sliding through his bow legs. It seemed like there was a four-foot gap inside from knee to knee.

The kids called him "Uncle Bud." I found out later he didn't have a degree, but he was, and still is, the best in the business. This man was good. He sincerely had kids at heart and put in long hours before school by picking up kids before school and coaching after. He opened up the school gym at night and was in the community on weekends.

I got in trouble in the fourth grade and was sent to a white counselor's office. I was sitting on the bench outside the counseling office all prepared to give this white counselor a hard time. Down the hall walks Uncle Bud and says, "Come in my office."

Man, I didn't know how to react. He had blown my whole tough-guy strategy. He sat me down and asked me what happened, gave me a good counsel and said, "I don't want to see you in here again because of trouble. Do you understand?"

I said, "Yes. Thanks, Mr. Dunlap."

He then told me to call him Uncle Bud.

Wow, what a difference from the message I had gotten from other counselors. I knew this man cared.

Don Ritchie, on the other hand, somehow showed up from out of nowhere that time when I was in the Castle Rock Jail. He was slim and well built and had the appearance of being educated. He walked with his head proudly in the air, cool and calm. He had the look of a well-rounded everything—teacher, politician, counselor, social worker—you name it. Later, he and I would become better friends.

My mind drifted on to Gary Bohall. Yeah, even a crazy white guy like Gary Bohall. He's a real role model. All the days he spent taking me to his white church and to his white house and making me eat his unseasoned white food, and listen to his bland white music. I guess he really was just trying to help while I was on the run. He met the test. He tried to give of himself to me… even if I could never take it.

And the men who worked at the Boys' Club teaching us boxing, track, pool, football, and life skills I hadn't even realized until now. For one dollar a year, most poor kids could afford to go there and I went in the afternoons all through elementary school and during the summer. I could never take any of their help, but that doesn't mean any of these men were less great.

It just means I was playing defense...not offense.

Before I slept the lights cracked on. Breakfast.

"Okay, convicts. Get in line." The search procedure was one that would allow us to leave the facility to perform our play. Cold hands poked and prodded, checking for drugs, weapons, any contraband that could help in an escape...or further a hard-working criminal's business.

Again, handcuffed and shackled, we were escorted onto a bus that slowly chugged its way toward the women's prison. It was show time. In a few short minutes, we would be performing the play we'd worked on for weeks.

"Hey, man, I wonder if Luella will come. It sure would be nice to see that fine brown sugar. Maybe she'll get a backstage pass.

"Brother, there aren't any backstage passes. Quit dreaming."

And so the bus conversation went. I listened with a strange feeling of *déjà vu*. This was the kind of talking we did in the junior high locker room: women and their body parts. The bus pulled into the women's prison and we were shuffled into a holding area where we had the pleasure of re-experiencing the searches we had just left behind. I felt anxious and irritated at the procedure. I was pumped and ready to do the play. Pumped and ready to feel some freedom and some normalcy.

But my expectations were just too high. It was prison. I had fooled myself. The only extraordinary thing that happened was that Roseanne, a woman I had known when I was still on the outside, recognized me. Right in the middle of the play, she started calling out my name. In the end, she was escorted out. I was glad.

The seriousness of the Black message was in my soul. Her

behavior was undignified and made a mockery of the whole thing.

On the way back to M.S., my mind returned to the whole idea of role models and what made them. My brother Thomas had written me a letter. His first and only. He was fifteen, two years younger than me. His girlfriend Ann was pregnant. I had introduced them. He wrote to ask my advice about whether to marry her. It seemed strange that he should write and ask me.

I was his older brother, but we had never been close. He was quiet, a shy kind of person. Always holding back, reluctant to join in. I remember watching TV once and they were doing the James Brown. All of us kids got up and danced, but not Thomas. That memory was a symbol in my mind of how Thomas was. Nearly the exact opposite of me.

I didn't know what I was going to tell him about Ann. It seemed like a lot of pressure.

What if he did what I said, just because I said it and then his whole life got messed up. Huh.

I wanted to be a great man in Thom's life, but I don't remember what I told him.

LOOK INSIDE

Look inside
So you can
See the outside.

Listen
So you can
Hear what's not being said.

Think
So you can
Know.

Touch
So you can
Feel.

Feel
So you can
Learn to live.

Promise Lee, 1977

TWENTY

I had been in M.S. for about nine months and Tom Armour had done his job. Like so many times before, I was handcuffed and shackled and herded into a van where I and my few bagged possessions were hauled off to another facility. This time I was headed to the Medium Security facility in Buena Vista, Colorado—a sleepy mountain village about two hours away from my hometown and an hour and a half from Cañon City.

It was good to be out in the fresh air, but the low-lying clouds and the dreariness of the day made it seem like even Mother Nature was enforcing confinement. Despite all the open space, I still felt closed in. As Thomas Hood once wrote, "No fruits, no flowers, no leaves, no birds, November!" That line says it all.

Inside the van I leaned my head against the window, feeling the outside cold seeping in through my forehead. I dozed in and out, waking every time the bumps in the road rattled the window and my teeth. As glad as I was to be outside of prison walls, it still seemed like it took a long time to get to Buena Vista.

When we finally arrived, the routine was the same: strip search, mug shots, fingerprints, monkey suits. It seemed as if the facility had prepared for our arrival. The halls were clean and quiet. No one was around to welcome us, just the guards who hustled us through the West Wing.

Whether it was dumb luck or whether Levy's reports included my fear of heights, I was just plain glad they gave me a cell on the ground floor. The clank of my cell door was a comfort and took the edge off being in a new place. A guard came and shoved the same first-day gourmet meal—a bologna sandwich and a cup of Kool-Aid—under the door. I didn't eat it. I just laid down on my bunk and slept. No rats this time.

Morning came and I awoke to the sound of cell doors opening. I sat up on my bed, trying to gather my senses. Why were the people on my tier passing my cell and my door was still sealed?

"Hey, tell the guard to crack this cell. Number sixteen," I told one of the convicts shuffling by in front of me. After about fifteen or twenty minutes, a man with new cowboy boots, blue jeans, and a ten-gallon hat came to my cell. He was holding a tray and just looking at me. I had never seen a man that close before with a handlebar mustache. It was huge and very black.

"My name is Mr. Pasquale. You won't be going to breakfast this morning with the other fish. You've got to stay in your cell for twenty-four hours." Then he dropped the tray and kicked it under the bars into the middle of my cell. He turned and left.

I glanced at the slop on the tray. Scrambled eggs, half cooked and slimy, sat on the plate. Watery stuff was running out of them and a film had formed over the ooze, telling me without checking that they were stone cold. My throat started to close up and I felt like puking. There was no decision to make here. I didn't eat.

"Hey, man, just be cool." A voice floated down from the tier above. "They want you to act a fool so they can teach you a lesson. Especially that prejudice screw. Man, he hates niggers. That's why they got him working here."

Even though I couldn't see him, I had a good feeling about the man connected to the floating voice. I don't know what it was, actually. He just seemed all right. His name was Li'l Jim and his cell was almost directly above mine. So on that long day we got acquainted. Having Li'l Jim to talk to sure helped to pass the time alone in my cell.

In the morning, the tier doors cracked and this time my cell opened along with the others. As soon as I could, I met up with Li'l Jim. I was surprised when I finally saw him. He was a light skinned, skinny little guy with a big Afro and fiery style. His Afro had a patch of gray in it, right in front. I wondered if he'd dyed it.

It turned out I had been right about the news of our arrival coming on the grapevine before we even got there. Li'l Jim had heard it.

And when it turned out that Larry was put up top near Li'l Jim, the talking started. Of course, Darrell White, who'd snitched on us, had been sent to Buenie right from sentencing.

"So what really went down, Promise?" Li'l Jim asked that first morning.

I wound up telling him the whole sorry story. "And I'm gonna kill Darrell," I finished, after I'd worked myself up.

"Well," Li'l Jim said like he was studying the matter. "I'm down with you." Li'l Jim and I always hung tight after that.

The walk to the chow hall that first morning out of my cell seemed like a mile, even though it was probably only one hundred feet. Everyone was checking me out. No doubt they knew, like Li'l Jim had known, who I was and where I came from. I watched the faces and caught a few eyes as I went by, but saw no challenges in the crowd, save one.

He came strolling along, apart from the crowd. A faggot walking along looking just like a woman. He wore his hair just so and had on feminine shoes. His outershirt had been made into a halter top. As he passed, his tongue slipped from between moist lips, circling them in a luscious, lazy fashion, as he looked me dead in the eye. A cold, hard, unflinching stare. I returned the glare, working the offense. My mind reviewed several schemes to entrap that queer. I didn't land on a definite plan right then, but I knew I'd eventually have me someone to do my laundry and get me commissary.

Breakfast was uneventful and after we ate, I was shuffled across the hall to have my head shaved. This was part of the incentive program. Right now, I was in the West Wing. That's where the Fish Tank was and the hole, a place I would find myself more than once. Inmates were promoted from wing to wing based on time served in each wing, behavior, and availability. You started in the West Wing, where you were in your cell all the time, except for one hour for meals and an hour a week of yard time. After that you could be promoted to the North, the South, and finally the East Wing. Ideally, you'd spend six weeks here, a couple of months there, always moving forward without getting sent back.

Promotion to each wing added privileges, like wearing civilian clothes, getting more yard time, and growing your hair. In the East Wing, the highest wing, they had cells with doors you could lock and unlock on your own. You got limited visitors. You could eat in the reformatory restaurant, stuff like that. It was like a little kiddy thing.

For now I was in the West Wing and the West Wing had only one hairstyle. Bald. And by the way, even after Li'l Jim got his head shaved, he never lost the gray patch in his hair. I guess it wasn't dyed after all.

Life at Buenie was boring. I studied for my GED and passed. Tom Armour had told me that if I got a trade, the parole board would be more likely to let me out. So I tried to sign up for the shortest trade course they had, meat cutting. They wouldn't let me into that one, which was only six months long, so I took the next shortest. Nine months of cooking. And beyond that, I took all the college they had available. I made it pretty much straight through to the East Wing and all its privileges. I only got sent back once for fighting.

I was thinking the whole time that if I did these things, they'd let me out. But the parole board just kept saying, "You're not ready. You're not ready." I gave up thinking that playing their game was going to get me out of the system completely, so I changed my tactic. I started writing, requesting to be sent back to Cañon City—not M.S., but to Max. It seemed like that would be the only place I could keep my mind busy and where it wasn't all a bunch of kid stuff. But they kept telling me, "No," on that too.

So I did what I could at Buenie to try to keep from being bored. I built myself a business. They called it racketeering, but I called it good offense.

The way it worked was like Popeye's friend, Wimpy. "I will gladly pay you Tuesday for a hamburger today." Every week I had visitors bringing me dope and other commodities. An inmate could "buy" stuff like cigarettes, cookies, or postage stamps today and pay for them on payday the next week. Stores could be either two-for-one or three-for-one. In other words, you repaid either two or three packs of cigarettes for the one you bought today. This was how the stores got their inventory.

My ability to run a profitable store gave me a lot of power in the joint. I never stole, but like the sandwich stuff at the grocery store so long ago, I did take whatever I wanted.

I not only got my "challenge faggot" to do laundry, but a bunch of others to work for me, too. In the East Wing you could have an iron and everybody liked to be *starched down*. So people came and gave me their shirts and a carton of cigarettes. I'd give the shirts to the fags to hand wash and use that liquid starch and then iron them.

When you had too much stuff in your cell, they knew you were running a store and doing other stuff. So to keep from being caught, I began franchising out. I had stores in all the wings, not just East. But they were still always trying to catch me doing something. Finally, one day they came to my cooking class. I had a joint on me. To keep from having it found on me, I threw it. But they saw me do it, so that's when they had me.

I went before the prison court, charged with racketeering and running a prostitution ring. I was also using the faggots to run an escort service there in the prison. I got busted back to the West Wing and sentenced to two weeks in the hole.

The word "assay" means to test by the application of pressure, as in applying air pressure to steel pipes to see whether or not they break or burst. If they do, they are discarded. The hole is designed much like this. The hole is a prison within a prison. You are in a dark cell twenty-four hours a day. It's called the hole because there is a hole in the middle of the dark cell that serves as your toilet. There is no bed or cot in the hole. You are given a blanket and sometimes a piece of foam pillow. The hole is located away from the rest of the prison population. No one can hear you yell, curse, or cry.

When the weather outside is cold, the hole is cold. When it's hot, the hole is hot. There is no light in the cell. The only time you see light is when your meals arrive. Because of darkness and seclusion several things occur. You hallucinate, talk to yourself, and sometimes feel things crawling on you. Many people have lost their minds in the hole. I have heard people say that it is better to be on death row because at least there you know the outcome. Many have gone into the hole tough and returned with mush minds. In the hole you could lose your mind and remain in your body. I don't know which is worse.

The prison system itself is the hole of society.

It's in solitary confinement that you really learn to appreciate the basic things of life, like meals. Getting your food is about the only diversion you get for your mind or your senses. And the guards are the only human faces you see. Of course, the guards know all that. And over the years, they develop their own ways of making your time in the hole even worse than it is. The same guard brought my meals to me every day, so it could have been okay. But instead of just coming and doing his job, he'd come to the door of the cell and just before sliding the meal tray in through the slot, he'd spit in my food. Right into my food.

He'd make some kind of snide comment like, "Got a little gift for you, Lee. Something to make your food a little sweeter." Then he'd land a big, slimy lugie right in the middle of the plate.

Those two weeks in Solitary were even harder, knowing that they still weren't going to send me back to Cañon City. My break would have to come soon. And it did.

At Buena Vista there was no common enemy for the convicts. It was the Mexicans against the Blacks, the Blacks against the Whites, the Whites against the System, the System against everybody.

One day a little race riot broke out. Everybody fighting everybody. Nobody got killed or anything, just fighting everywhere. I was charged with instigating the riot and was finally okayed to be sent back to Cañon. I was part of the riot, but I didn't start anything. But I didn't care. Guilty or not, I was going to get what I wanted out of the deal, so I stayed on the offense and didn't offer even a sentence in my own defense. I played the game and kept it cool.

So once again, I found myself handcuffed and shackled and loaded into a van. I wondered if Dr. Levy would be glad to see me.

Twenty-One

"Hey, Promise Lee. Man, is that you? Where have you been?" Those questions repeated over and over again, let me know I was truly home. That I had been missed. That I was the "Godfather" and my family was here waiting for me.

Even the system seemed to be giving me a welcome home gift. No Fish Tank. This time they sent me straight back behind the walls to Cellhouse Seven—Maximum Security at the Colorado State Penitentiary in Cañon City.

I walked hard, carrying only my roll back into the cellhouse. I was Black, I was strong, I was invincible, and I was ready to play whatever hand I was dealt... and win.

"How long since you been here, man?" A voice floated to my ears, but I saw no one. A strange sense of familiarity came over me. Stronger than just being home. It was the voice. I turned around and there was Li'l Jim.

"Damn, man!" I greeted him. "I didn't think I'd ever see you again once you left Buenie."

"Yeah. You knew they bumped me up here a few months ago. But how 'bout you, Promise? The word here is that you been gone a long time."

The fact was that it did seem like a long time. The time in Buenie had been hard for me, maybe because I had been learning the ropes. Those changes were a struggle for me. On the one hand, I was fighting and becoming an angry, no-nonsense, kill-at-the-drop-of-a-hat convict. On the other hand, if I was to survive my sentence, it didn't seem like I could become anything but that. Making that transformation seemed the right thing to do. But it made me angry on the inside and that showed on the outside.

"Brother, it's only been a year and a half. Not that long." I nodded my head toward the brother standing next to Jim. He looked familiar.

"P, this here's Zambizi."

I nodded to Zambizi. "Yeah, man. I remember you from the Fish Tank."

"That's right, bro. 1974. The joint lucked out that year. They got us both."

"Amen, brother. It was a very good year. But you know, I thought your name was Jason X, man."

"It was. I changed it. It's time I paid tribute, you know. To those who were in the struggle before it was a struggle."

"Hey, man, we knew you were coming so we got you a place. There's a cell open on third tier between Zambizi and me. Come on."

Knowing both Jim and Jason X, it seemed strange that they would have hooked up. They were completely different. Jason X was a serious guy. Jim liked to joke and tease. But as I learned in my first few days back in the walls, they had three things in common— doin' time, boxing, and the ability to kill without flinching.

So there we were, three killers in a row. Jim and Jason X brought me up to date on who was who and what was what. As they did, I had a growing sense of the inevitable. I'd be tested and tried. In order to live, I'd probably have to take a life. The good thing about it was that unlike Buenie, where you could get five years for a fight, in Cañon, most of the time killing went unpunished.

Yeah, this was nothing like Buenie or M.S. It was Max. The graveyard. And I was glad to be back.

The who-was-who part of things was always easy for me, so it didn't take long for everyone who hadn't known me to know me. I started to settle into the new routine.

They gave me a choice. I could work making license plates and earn thirty cents per day or do nothing and earn seven cents per day. I chose to earn the seven cents and put my energy elsewhere.

"Hey, Promise. We're going to work out tonight. Wanna come?"

"Yeah," I said rolling off of my bunk. "I'm ready for a change of scenery."

Boxers were given special privileges. Ron Lyle was a pro who fought Ali. He had put Cañon on the map and they wanted to continue the reputation. Boxers had a lot more access to the yard, the kitchen, and the gym.

As we walked toward the gym, I thought about Harvey Banks and "the worm." I promised myself I'd never be a fool like that again. But at the same time, I knew that I'd been blessed with fast and powerful hands. After all, I'd been knocking dudes out on the street as long as I could remember.

Prison gyms are like all others, a feast for the senses. As soon as you enter, you are struck by a unique smell that is the combined odors of sweat and tennis shoes. And the sounds, like the squeaking of sneakers on the floor and the echoing voices, are larger than life. The high ceilings rain down artificial light and the metal stairs leading down to the gym floor resound with jogging footsteps, anxious to vent their tension and excess energy.

This night, however, the gym was nearly empty. "Come on, Promise. Let's see what you got," Jason prodded. "Spar with me." I declined, preferring to watch instead.

Jason and Jim messed around for a while, then Jason asked again, "Come on, man. Let's not lose the opportunity. Come on in the ring." Then he added with a slow kind of sly smile, "I ain't gonna hurt you."

Even though Jason and I were all right, I knew his look was a for-real kind of challenge. So friend or no friend, I gloved up and climbed into the ring. Someone rang the bell and I popped out of my corner. I really didn't want to hurt him, but you can bet I wasn't going to get hurt either.

It took only a few seconds for me to size up his moves, then I made mine. In just a few more seconds I was landing blows at will. Upper cuts, jabs, hooks. Jason's body was my oyster.

At the first-round bell, it seemed like everyone in the gym was in my corner telling me how to hurt Jason. "Nah, man. He's my partner. Give me someone else." Finally, a couple of old guys pushed through. I recognized them as the boxing trainers, Dennis and Horse.

Horse spoke real soothingly into my ear, "No, son. Take off your gloves for now. I want you to meet me here in the gym tomorrow morning. Then we'll see what you really got."

The following morning I got my first official introduction to the trainers. Both were former boxers. Horse was also a martial artist and a medical doctor. That morning we started my real training as a boxer, not just a hack. Dennis worked on making me ringwise. Horse drove me like a horse to get in shape. I learned "quick kill" techniques and how to really hurt someone or take them out. With their wisdom and my natural speed and power, I was knocking folks out at will. But every blessing has its burden. Within weeks, no one would get in the ring with me except the heavyweights. And even though I could bench press 325 pounds, I was only 165.

In my time in the joint, someone once told me, "Learn all you can and can all you learn." In other words, use it. This was easy enough in boxing when you immediately got to test out a new style or technique. What you learned in your head could become real in your hands in just a few minutes.

But in real life, in the Pen, the last part of the saying was just a little hard. I read and studied. I listened and thought. I dreamed and prayed. But still, I was in the Pen and my ideas and hopes were still just in my head. I was a rabbit in a snare, unsure if I'd die in the trap or if some people outside of my control would set me and my dreams free.

When I sat in my cell and thought about my reality, it was almost more than I could bear. So I looked forward to yard time—to being able to go to the gym and to have a connection to something real and tangible.

When I got there, I took a long breath, and quietly surveyed the men in the gym, moody and alone with my thoughts.

"Hey, man, I been thinking about your right hook."

I let my breath out with a loud, disgusted sigh, but Dennis didn't notice. He just kept on. "It just still ain't right. Now, what you need to do is...."

"Maaaan... Shut Up! What makes you think you know anything about me or my right hook? You're just an old man trying to relive your glory days through me." I turned my back on him, knowing it was an all-out insult and sign of disrespect.

"Okay. So you think you're a tough guy? Well, I've had enough of your prima donna mess. You think you know so much, get your behind in the ring and you can teach me."

Why did he have to start bugging me now? I just wanted to work out and think. To be left alone with just me and my training. "Okay," I relented. "I don't want to hurt you man, but you're leaving me no choice."

Dennis was already gloving up and climbing into the ring. The other men were gathering around and chattering like there was a schoolyard fight brewing.

I took my time and strolled over to the ring. I was pissed at Dennis, but at the same time I didn't want to hurt him. He was an old man—probably close to forty-five—and my trainer. Two good reasons why I shouldn't get in the ring with him, even if he didn't know anything on anything.

"Look, man, I don't want to fight you," I argued even as I climbed into the ring.

"Your hands better be up at the bell," he warned. And at that instant the bell rang DING.

I came out of the corner, instantly jabbing him at will. He kept coming, so I danced, jabbed, hooked, even hit him with some upper cuts.

DING. DING.

"You had enough, old man?" I yelled from my corner.

"You're leaving yourself open for hooks," he called back.

"Well, why aren't you hooking me then?" I jeered.

DING

I jabbed the old man a few more times. Then, suddenly, I didn't know where I was. Everything was spinning. There was a turtle sitting on a rock, playing a banjo and bells were ringing all around like in a church. I heard a voice say, "That's enough." It was Dennis.

"No, wait. We ain't finished."

"No, man. You've had enough. I didn't mean to hurt you, bro."

"Give me another round," I demanded.

DING.

Fists were flying everywhere, and I had the sense that I was not in complete control of my body. It was on automatic pilot. I was trying to fall, but I couldn't.

My head was numb. I was sure I was tasting blood. Now I wanted it to end. Where was the bell? My arms flailed and I knew that even in that state, I made contact at least one more time, but I didn't care. I just wanted it to end.

DING. DING. DING. DING.

"You had enough man?" he asked, not unkindly.

"Yeah, man. I have."

It took all my strength to get back to my cell, fronting like I was just fine. After a while I puked and that made me feel a little better. Some of the guys sent kind words. What I thought was going to be an embarrassment for Dennis turned out to be an Excedrin headache for me.

"Hey, man, don't you know Dennis had one of the deadliest hooks in the game?"

"I do now," I said, laughing it off.

But that's why he had wanted to teach me so badly. I guess he felt he had one more thing to teach me and I guess I was ready to learn this one more lesson. I hated that I had to learn it the hard way. But you can bet my right hook was never the same.

It was 1976. I was eighteen. There hadn't been a lockdown in weeks. No riots. No shankings. The holidays were coming on. The tension and electricity in the air were so thick, our hair practically stood on end. Everybody knew something had to give and give soon. So without a suitable alternative, our focus was on the fight card Dennis and Horse were putting together.

I couldn't wait.

"Hey, bro," Horse called as I jogged down the stairs to the gym. We're putting together a fight card for next month. You're down to fight Hererra."

"Hererra?"

"Yeah, the one that don't hardly speak English."

"Come on Horse, what kind of ticket is that?"

"That's your ticket, bro. Take it or leave it," and he turned and walked away.

Despite my rather unfortunate bout with Dennis, my fame among the welterweights had grown. The whole penitentiary, and even the folk at M.S., knew I'd been having trouble finding enough convicts to fight. No one wanted to mess with me.

So even a full sixty days before the fight, the bets were being laid on our card. Mexicans for Hererra and Blacks for me. Among the boxers there was usually a lot of camaraderie, but when it came right down to it, when the tension was this high and when lines had to be drawn, it was the whites with the whites, the Muslims with the Muslims, and the Blacks with the Blacks. That's how the betting went.

"What you say, P? You gonna win?"

"Damn, man. Of course I'm gonna win. I'll have him bloody as a pig. As a matter of fact, if I don't win, whatever you bet, I'll pay you double. If I win, you don't owe me nothing."

"Man, I'll take that action."

"Me, too."

The bets on that action spread down the tier like gasoline on fire. There was nothing to lose.

Carwell, a friend from the tier, pulled me aside. "Man, you're doing the wrong thing. If you lose, these folks are going to want their money. That's gonna start a riot...."

I looked him dead in the eye. Silent. I turned and walked away, never saying anything.

I knew I could beat Hererra with my eyes closed. In the Pen, there's only so much space. So when I was running, Hererra was running. When he was sparring, I was too. I knew him and I knew me. I was better.

But Carwell was right. I shouldn't have shot my mouth off.

Time slowed to a crawl the days and weeks before the fight. I was eager to further my reputation.

TWENTY-TWO

Call me old-fashioned, but I believe in the wisdom of old adages and proverbs. Take the one that says, "You can never go home." To hear the folks tell it, that saying means that things never stay the same and when you try to go back, you'll be disappointed because you can't relive any part of your life.

That's when you know you're growing up. When you try to go back and have this realization that things are different…for good.

Somehow I had gotten it into my mind that coming back to Cañon City would make everything all right. But the fact was it had been over four years since my sentencing. The letters had dwindled to a trickle. Visits had stopped. I was completely out of touch with the outside world and bored with the inside one.

The joint held no more challenges for me. Everything had become routine. The riots, the shootings, the food, the boxing. Everything. I was burnt out and feeling old. At twenty, I wasn't the youngest inmate anymore. The title, Little Brother, that I had hated so much and then come to accept, was now only a memory. Nobody called me that anymore. I had graduated into being a real convict. Now, instead of folks seeking me out to give advice, they came to get it. I thought about the men of influence who had been in the news lately. Nine hundred Jim Jones cult members had died in Guyana in a murder-suicide. Now *that* was a powerful leader. Pope Paul II was beginning his reign after two other popes died, one right after the other. He would be powerful, too, but in a whole different way. They were powerful in their worlds. I was powerful in mine.

Over the years I had met with the parole board several times, but each time the answer was the same: "You're not ready." So I got in a mindset of just doing time and for the first time, wondering why I was in the Pen and if I was really guilty.

About this same time, a guy we called Flip on the streets came behind the walls. His real name was Charles Smalls and long ago he had been my crime mentor. We had run together and he had proven himself to be a worthy con man, thief, and fighter. Now he had drawn a double life sentence for murder.

When I first saw him, I felt the joy of seeing something familiar, like the Christmas decorations each year. Something you've seen a hundred times before, but it's just a sight for sore eyes because it reminds you of family and being happy and of everything real in life. That's how I felt when I saw Flip.

Still though, I was sorry to see him under those circumstances. And even though he was a bit of home, I kept my distance. He hadn't done time before and was just getting ready to experience all the things I had already gone through and they were bittersweet. I just couldn't handle it, so I just kept completely away. Man, what was going on in my mind?

Because of the racism and prejudiced actions of the parole board, most of the brothers and Mexicans were boycotting parole hearings. They figured that if you were just going to be told no, why humiliate yourself by asking "the man" for freedom in the first place?

I was up to meet the Board again in a few weeks. My mind and heart were twisted over the issue. Should I go to meet the Board or just stay in for two more years and kill my number? Then, on a day in August, or maybe it was September, it happened. I was on my way back to the cellhouse from an evening workout in the gym. When I had gone in, earlier in the day, it had been light out. But now, all of a sudden, for the first time in the four years since I was put in county jail I saw stars. I saw the stars!

The night was clear, the air was fresh, and the sky was all twilight and bluish black. And it seemed like every star had my name on it, was one of my dreams just waiting to become real, waiting for me to see it, waiting for me to happen to look up and find it. They were all there, waiting for me. All I had to do was reach for them.

But before any of that could happen, I had to get out of this place. God had spoken to me again.

"Guard! Can I go see Dr. Levy?" He didn't answer. He just kept doing his count. "Please, I'd like to see the doctor," I called down the tier after him.

After a couple of days, they gave me a pass to Levy's office. I really knew I was an old con then because they sent me unescorted.

Everything about Levy and his office was the same. The same cinderblock hall. The same waiting bench outside. The same small, gray, untidy man. Everything uniquely nondescript and colorless.

The head game was the same, too. Even though I had an appointment, I waited on the bench for over an hour. Finally, I heard Levy's footsteps on the stairs. I watched him stroll nonchalantly down the hall and right past me without saying a word. I watched him go into his office and I watched the sliver of his office, visible in the doorway, disappear as he closed the door behind him.

Outside on the bench, I continued to wait. Another half hour passed without being called into his office. Slightly nervous, I got up and knocked on the door. Again I waited, but heard no answer. So I knocked a second time and for a second time got no response. Slowly I eased the door open just a crack. Levy was sitting at his desk reading. He didn't look up, just grumbled "What?" The pipe dangling from his lip flipped up and down as he said it.

"I'm meeting the parole board and I want a recommendation from you to the Board. A positive recommendation."

"Why, Lee? Why should I do that for you? So you can kill again? So you can get out and murder someone else? Lee, you're a convict. I ought to kill you like you killed the others. You want me to kill you, Lee?"

"Dr. Levy, thank you for your time." I turned my back on him and walked out.

"Close my door. Close my door, Lee. You opened it! See, you're nothing but a convict!"

I just continued to walk, never looking back.

"Mr. Lee, you've been here for a little over four years now and by your presence, you're indicating you wish to be paroled. Am I correct?"

"Yes, I am."

"You've had a number of write-ups, most of them having to do with violence and a lack of respect toward authority. In fact, you've even been implicated as an instigator of two riots and the knife-man in three stabbings, two of which have resulted in death. You've threatened the life of guards, administrators, and even our chief psychiatrist, Dr. Levy. Why? Tell me, why in God's name should we let you go? You're a danger to society as well as a disgrace. You haven't learned your lesson. You've only learned how to be a better con. And I don't mean convict! I mean con man. Before the Board dismisses you, do you have anything to say?"

"Yes. I want not just you, but the entire Board to know some things. I committed a crime. In the eyes of some, an unforgivable crime. I took a life."

"I came in here as a boy, a kid, a fifteen-year-old kid. I have been robbed of my childhood. I didn't go to the senior prom like most kids do. I didn't get a chance to be big brother to my sister and brothers. I didn't take graduation pictures."

"Being in here, I have been forced to grow from boy to man in order to survive. I have had to live by the principle of "kill or be killed." I know what I did was wrong. But for me to stay in here will only make me bitter and you will be guilty of nurturing a criminal. You will make me into a career criminal.

"In here I will grow bitter and cold and begin to hate society. Leaving me in here will give me a bad taste in my mouth for white men in suits and women who wear neckties. I ask you to consider how much harm you will do by perpetuating my incarceration.

"If I am not released this time, you will become guilty of crimes far greater than mine. You become guilty of creating a man that hates the look and sound and smell of authoritative white people."

"So the decision is yours. You can give me the opportunity to become a productive citizen of this society or force me to become anti-American, anti-white, anti-law, and worst of all, anti-love."

A deathly silence, punctuated with fear and amazement, gripped the room. I studied their faces and could see their silent gasping as if the air had suddenly turned thick and clogged their throats. For me, it was the first time in a long time that I breathed free.

Levy was in the corner, but his look was a little different. Some of his grayness was gone and there was actually a look of sanity about him. He didn't say a word, just hung his head. This was the first time since I'd known him that he seemed like he had some sense. Like he knew he was guilty and felt ashamed of his past behavior.

I trusted that the Board would do the right thing. Not because they were capable of doing good, but because they were incapable of doing anything that wasn't in their own interest.

They knew I could do another year and kill my number. That would afford me the luxury of not having a parole officer. Upon release, I would be able to go anywhere I wanted to. Even to the city where they lived. Even to the stores where they shopped. Even to the schools their children attended. Even to their homes.

They realized that if I killed my number, I could be anywhere. And the two places they didn't want me were in their lives or in their heads.

"Lee," the Parole Board spokesman said as he cleared his throat. "Your release will be strongly based on your psychological profile. You're dismissed."

I got up out of my chair and proceeded to the exit. When I got close enough to the door to push it open, I slowly turned around. Then, nodding that imperceptible nod that indicates you recognized a person or situation for what it is, I said, "Thank you for your time."

I walked back to the cellhouse strong and erect. I knew I had shot my best shot and it felt good. I had meant what I said and knew it was the truth. And this truth had set me free in mind, if not in body.

As I moved along the walkways back to the cellhouse, I had the unearthly feeling that I existed outside of my body. That I was up above, watching the flesh and blood that humankind called Promise Lee. Even from that distance I saw he was a man who could operate in many worlds. Black and white, bound and free, physical and mental, emotional and intellectual. I saw a man who was the product of his environment, but this fact had caused him to become ruler of his own destiny. Was he a man with a past but no future? Or was he a man with a future unbounded by his past?

TWENTY-THREE

"Hey, man. How'd it go?" Li'l Jim asked. "Just the usual," I replied. I'd been to the Board every six months or so since I came in. "If I have to, I'm going to kill my number. I'm not going before the Board again. Levy was in there."

"What? That means they're going to deny you. Did he say anything?"

"No. He didn't even look at me."

"That means they're going to turn you down."

"It don't matter. If I have to, I'll kill this number. Let's go to chow."

On the way back from dinner a man they called Tudlum pulled me aside. "Hey, man, it's going to be some stuff." I didn't ask any questions about what was going on or who the beef was with. We just got strapped. If you did ask, it was a sign of weakness. Most cons had shanks about three to six inches long. We did, too, but we also had swords. We had gotten metal pieces from music stands and handles from dippers and spatulas. Our swords were as long as our arms.

I had outgrown the joy of the hunt and was now only concerned with the kill. That's why we soaked the tips of our shanks in feces. I had been told it would enter the blood stream and kill a man slowly but surely. I had concluded that Li'l Jim's assessment of my parole board hearing was probably correct. So if I was going to stay until I could leave without their consent, I at least wanted to leave alive. A couple of weeks passed, though, without action in the cellhouse or word from the Board.

So I remained alert.

We had just finished lunch and were standing on the bottom floor toward the back of the cellhouse. Anytime I was strapped, that was where you could find me. It was the best and safest place to be. You could see the movements of most of the guards, in case you needed to dump your shank. Being on the first floor, there was no risk of being thrown off a tier in a fight. And, as I had learned years ago, no one can watch your back like the wall. Not even your closest brother or friend.

So I was standing there on alert when I heard someone shout, "Man down."

Instantly it was pure chaos. The cons were running around like ants. I flashed back to being about six or seven years old and living in Texas. There were huge ant hills, perhaps a foot or more high, with thousands of ants spilling over the edges of their portals, scurrying in every direction at once. As a small boy, they offered endless intrigue and opportunities for exploration. And the hotter it was, the more active the hills seemed to become.

I was playing on such a hill one summer day with my brother Thomas. We were inserting twigs into the holes of the ant hill to extract chains of ants. Once outside their nests, we would stomp them before they could sting us and keep us from further invasions. Here we had happily played the morning away and were just beginning to wonder about lunch and peanut butter sandwiches, when we heard our mother's long and wailing screams.

Thomas and I dropped our sticks and ran headlong for the house. There, in the kitchen, my mother alternately wept and screamed. We strained our ears to catch the few garbled words that tumbled from her lips. I felt as helpless as I had when Ms. Sheppard had cried so pitifully.

"It's okay, Mommy," I said, touching her long soft hair with my fingertips. Still sitting in the kitchen chair, she leaned toward me and held me tight. For the first time, I could understand her sorrowful words, whispered huskily into my ear, "He's deaf."

Of course, I knew she meant my baby brother, Thurmas. My dad was stationed out of the country, so she had packed up me and Thomas and Charmas and the baby with a burning fever and set off on the train for "home." She wanted to see the family doctor when the Air Force doctors couldn't tell her why Thurm was so sick—why his fever wouldn't go down, why his neck was stiff as a board. Now she had the answer she had come for. Thurm had meningitis.

When I came out of my daydream, I saw the same scene here in prison. Everybody was scrambling to get to a different somewhere.

"Lockdown! Lockdown!" The announcement came over the loudspeaker and the guards yelled it out as well.

This meant that everyone had to go to their own cell and when the door cracks open, go in and stay there for count. It took just a minute for the guards to crack our doors and when they did, we threw our shanks over the third-tier rail. Their landing sounded like a ton of fifty-cent pieces falling from the top of a skyscraper.

We stayed on lockdown for two weeks, but it seemed like forever. Man, that's hard time. Boxing was over with and the tension seemed to just get thicker and thicker.

During all this time, I still had no word from the parole board. It had been four weeks since I'd met with them and made my case. Zambizi came up for parole, but he refused to see the Board. He had a forty-year sentence and he was determined to kill his number. That would mean he'd have to do about twenty years if he received good time. How could a man do twenty years and expect to function on the streets? How could a man do a year and expect to function on the streets?

TWENTY-FOUR

"Hey, man, heard the news. Congratulations!" Li'l Jim was his same wired, high-energy self. "What's the first thing you're gonna do when you get out? Get some trim? Buy you a stash?"

"Nah, man. It's gonna take me a while. They won't release me to Colorado."

"No? Where you going?"

"Texas. Houston, Texas."

"What's in Texas 'cept a bunch of cows?"

"Nah, it ain't that bad. My family's there."

Li'l Jim persisted in his interrogation, but it was making me sick. The more he talked about the outside world, the more the panic rose inside of me. What was I going to do? How was I going to make a living with a cooking certificate that said ISSUED BY THE COLORADO STATE DEPARTMENT OF CORRECTIONS in bold print right on the front of it?

"Look, Jim, I appreciate your enthusiasm, but could you just shut the hell up?" Jim's eyebrows slanted toward his nose and his eyes looked sorrowful, like a puppy that had just been kicked. But right now I didn't care how I made him feel.

I just laid down on my bunk to think. This was my home. This is where I had been raised. These men were my mentors, my teachers, and my family. Here I was respected by all and honored by most. I had survived insurmountable odds. I was a legend in my own time, a hero, a boy who had been destined to die but who, by determination, had lived. I had survived not only as a human, but had succeeded as a man.

Was I to leave my friends in here to suffer the harsh realities that go along with survival? Could I desert those who had mentored me? Those who taught me how to deal with racial, social, and economic oppression? Weren't they my family now? Isn't it "one for all and all for one"?

And what about those who now looked up to me as the example? Should I leave them here in the hands of wolves? Did I have a responsibility to them?

I don't even know my biological family any more. Even Jesus asked, "Who is my mother and who are my brothers?" He asked because his real family didn't know his pain or his suffering. Mine didn't understand either. Sure, they knew me as a young child, but they don't know me now. They don't know I'm a killer, more than once. They don't know I have no reservations about taking a life. They don't know I have become an animal—one that can turn from kid to killer in the blink of an eye. They don't know my pain. They don't know my suffering. They don't know my rage. Simply put, they don't know me.

There was both sadness and happiness about my departure. Some were happy, so they could be the new king, but mostly, those who knew me wanted to see me make it.

I had just fourteen days until my out date, November 22, 1978. But the tension continued to build. It was always like that around holiday time. Everyone felt the stress, just like on the outside.

Li'l Jim was on the hit list and I was in the middle. The beef was between Li'l Jim and a longtimer. As it turns out, the men who rode with the longtimer were good friends of mine, too. So like I said, I was caught in the middle.

The longtimer's friends came to see me and said, "You parole in a few days. Now you know Li'l Jim and you know that you're the one that's been keeping him alive. Nobody else likes him. This thing is going down and you don't need to be in it. Do you understand?"

"What you don't understand," I said, "is that I stand with Li'l Jim. Now and until I leave… if I leave. Him and I are riding together. You know, it's got to be what it's got to be. That's where I stand."

Even just days before my out date, I found myself strapped. Jim, Jason and I watching each other's backs. A Black guard came to me and told me he knew what was going down and that I should stay clean.

"Thanks for the advice," I told him.

But in my heart and mind I stood with Li'l Jim till the end. The situation ended in the yard, with the three of us against nine of them. I was able to squash the whole thing by revealing that it was simply a misunderstanding. This rarely happens in prison because of egos, attitudes, and reputations to uphold. But it did this time. I was able to diplomatically negotiate a truce without us appearing weak.

Some of the things you see in the movies are made up junk, but some things are for real. It was my turn now to actually experience what it was like to get the proverbial suit of clothes, a few dollars in your pocket, and be put out on the street, the prison gates locking behind you and you on the outside.

This time, with no handcuffs and no shackles, they loaded me into a nondescript government car to drive me to the bus station. There is a saying in the Pen, "Never look back." It means that when they finally let you out, don't look back at the Pen because if you do, you'll come back again. As the car pulled away, I decided I wouldn't be bound by superstition. I looked back and it felt good, but it felt strange at the same time.

The guards were supposed to buy my bus ticket and then give me one hundred dollars "out" money, but they seemed hell-bent on doing me one last injustice. They used my hundred dollars to buy my bus ticket and handed me just a few cents change. That and the twenty-three dollars from my account were supposed to make my new start in life.

Walking out on the street was almost unbearable. It seemed like everyone was looking at me. And the truth is, they were.

The suit of clothes they gave me to wear out of the Pen was ancient history. The guards had taken me into a little room filled with clothes to let me pick out what I wanted to wear. But the fact was that all the clothes were all out of style, maybe from the late sixties.

So it wasn't the fault of the people on the street. My polyester pants with little flower-like things around the bell bottoms were probably worthy of a stare.

And my hair, too. Even though I'd grown my hair out, it was still in marked contrast to the styles most brothers were wearing. I hadn't been that self-conscious about my hair since sixth grade at Sacred Heart Academy, the year I was selected to do my turn as altar boy during mass. Now, I had justly earned a reputation for cutting up in class, so all the kids thought I was just clowning around when the candle I was carrying lit my huge, blown-out Afro on fire. I had never meant to do it. It was truly an accident. But I certainly had the attention of my classmates who laughed and jeered for days afterwards.

Now I had the attention of everyone on the street and at the Greyhound bus terminal.

"How long is it to Houston?" I asked the ticket clerk.

"About thirty hours, son. Hope you like to ride."

The fact was, at that moment, I didn't like anything at all. After being confined for that long, the wide-open spaces seemed like just that, open space. I felt like an astronaut space walking. Connected to nothing in the universe except a little lifeline. In my case, that lifeline was the tiny thread, linking my past to those stars I'd seen some nights ago, all my hopes and dreams. And it was a thread. A threadbare thread. One likely to break at any moment.

I took deep breaths to calm myself and checked out the scenery. The town of Cañon City was an old one and the bus station was located in the heart of downtown. The quaint main street district was bustling with its residents, all proper, upstanding citizens finely dressed. Cars were lined up along the streets and all the parking meters had been duly plugged. The store windows advertised hardware and dresses and the latest fashion in shoes. The bank had a "Welcome! Come In, We're Open" sign out front. Of course, I knew that didn't mean me. None of the welcome signs or window displays meant me.

I sat on the bench outside the ticket window at the bus station. The fumes from idling buses were stifling. Even though my bus didn't leave for a long time, I hung around close by. I didn't want to take the chance of missing it. After all, it was my way out of town. Plus, the guards who had brought me were hanging around to make sure I got on the bus.

Finally, a uniformed driver showed up at the door of the waiting bus and announced that the Number Fifteen bound for Pueblo and Dallas was ready for boarding. This was it. I tried to act particularly casual as I strode over to the open bus door.

As I got ready to board, the world seemed to stand still. My mind flashed back to the many times before when I had been loaded onto a van against my will, bound with handcuffs and shackles. A stallion driven away from the open range to life in a corral.

This time I had the advantage of going to a familiar place, of knowing the folks there, and the lay of the land on the other end of the journey. I focused on this thought and took more deep breaths as the door shut behind me. It wasn't exactly the clanking of metal bars, but there was some comfort in it. The door was closing out the outside world for at least a little longer.

It wasn't until we actually rolled into Pueblo that I recalled the bus driver saying we'd stop. For just a brief moment, I felt excitement surge within me. Pueblo was only about thirty-five miles from Colorado Springs and I used to have some contacts here. Maybe I could get hooked up....

I hopped off the last step of the bus and onto the pavement. I looked around, scanning the streets for action, something I could sink my teeth into. I saw a pay phone and headed straight for it to see who I could scrape up. I put a dime in the phone and had just started to dial, when I heard a recorded voice say my call couldn't be completed. I tried it again. Then a third time. Again I felt the eyes of the world upon me, so I gave up.

And then, although it wasn't exactly the kind of action I had in mind, I saw her. She was the most homely beauty I had ever seen. And she was looking right at me with a coy little smile. More than my emotions were rising now.

The last of the bus passengers were just getting off and those staying in Pueblo were getting their luggage. "Twenty minutes," I heard the driver call. More than enough time, I thought, looking at my queen. More than enough time.

On the way out of town, I watched the scenery and tried not to appear too twitchy. In my head I knew there were no buildings in Pueblo more than three stories tall. But against the blueness of the sky, they seemed almost like skyscrapers. The more time passed, the more I knew this would be an incredibly long trip. You see, there is no way to sleep when there is no one to watch your back. No one you trust, not even the seat. So the weariness settled in, giving me space to figure out that phone calls now cost twenty cents. Man, I had been locked up a long time.

My folks had been notified of my release and were expecting me. Mom and Daddy had moved to Houston a few years earlier when Daddy retired from the Air Force. His family was from Houston and my mom's family was from Louisiana, just a few hours' drive away, so it was convenient for both of them, I guess. They had written me that Daddy was working for the gas company now.

As the bus droned on, I let my mind run free, trying to visualize how it was going to be—working on developing my offense. But as I thought about Texas, the only image I could get in my mind was going there as a little boy.

The slowing of the bus helped to pull my mind back to the reality of the trip. We were entering the city and I stretched, momentarily glad to consider getting off the bus, more permanently sickened at the thought of really having to face the outside world. I stepped off the bus and headed for the terminal. I guess I had nothing to do but call the folks and have them come get me.

Knowing this time that the phone took twenty cents, I was confident in my abilities. But when I got my dad on the phone, things seemed to go downhill. No mater how hard I tried, I couldn't make him understand where the terminal was. I gave him the cross streets, but everything was pure confusion.

After a while I looked up at the sign displaying the arrival and departure schedules. Letting my breath go, I closed my eyes in disbelief. I was in Dallas, not Houston. None of the street names were familiar because I was still hundreds of miles away.

Reluctantly, I confessed the mix-up to my dad. My worst fears were coming true. How was I going to make it in the outside world? I was twenty years old and I couldn't ride a bus. If I couldn't even make a phone call without messing up, how was I going to make a life?

Senses

Look in order to hear
Listen so you can see
Smell in order to taste
Feel so you can know quiet.
Now speak.
Now you live.

Promise Lee, 1978

TWENTY-FIVE

My temples throbbed and my eyes burned. I had stayed awake the entire way to Houston, trying to get used to being on the outside. I was tired. Mighty tired.

When the bus turned into the terminal, I began looking for whoever had been sent to pick me up, but I couldn't make out any familiar faces. I could feel the nervousness rising in me again, so I focused on staying calm and just getting off the bus. I didn't mind waiting for the other passengers to get off first. They were just giving me a few more moments to compose myself.

I may have just as well been on death row walking to the chair for all the effort it took to move my feet forward, down the aisle, and out the bus door.

Now, where were they? I still didn't see anyone I knew, so I walked around for a while. Still alone, I sat down on the long row of seats equipped with pay TVs. Someone had gotten up with some time still on the set, so I pretended to watch it. I didn't recognize the show, which was fine, because I didn't want to be distracted.

I had just gotten settled into my seat when I looked up and saw them walking toward me—Daddy and my brother Thomas.

"Hello, son."

I smiled and nodded. Thomas didn't say anything either.

"Ready to go?"

I nodded again and followed his lead to the little Ford Pinto that waited outside. When we got to the car, Thomas opened the passenger door and pulled the seat back forward, motioning for me to get in. In the back, that is. So we all piled in and headed for home.

"Well, son, how are you?"

"Fine, Dad. Fine."

Thom finally spoke. "How was the trip?"

"Fine, Thom. Just fine."

"Are you hungry?"

"A little."

"Well, your mom has made a big dinner. Turkey and every-thing."

"Good. That's real nice."

"The weather here's been unseasonably warm."

"Uh-huh."

And so the conversation went. Elementary questions and short, direct answers. It wasn't that I didn't want to be friendly. I could tell they were glad to see me and that made me feel a little more at ease, but I really wanted to concentrate on the scenery and getting the lay of the land. It was clear the city had really grown. We passed street after street of huge buildings and then got on a busy freeway. I knew I was in a part of town I'd never seen before.

We traveled north from downtown and finally exited onto a street that made my heart pound and my headache abruptly stop. Wall to wall, it was lined with pimps and whores, hole-in-the-wall clubs, liquor stores, and Cadillacs sporting sunroofs and wheel kits. Man, it was exciting. In my stomach I knew that eventually this was where I'd end up. This was Jensen Drive.

We followed the drive almost to the end and then turned left onto Turner. I could tell we were almost home by how slow Daddy was driving. The houses along Turner were pretty large and to my sur-prise most had goats or chickens or even cows in the front yard. I chuckled to myself. We had just turned off the most happening street in the city and now we were passing farm animals. I just sat back and marveled as this new world went by.

Finally we pulled up in front of a white house that sat on what I judged to be almost an acre of land, but this time there were no ani-mals in the front yard. No animals, that is, except for one. Just one. It was Caesar, my Dobe, who stood at the gate like a soldier on patrol. So he had survived, too!

Caesar and a red female puppy named Cleopatra had been Mom and Dad's last-ditch effort to straighten me out the summer before I went to jail. What memories. That was the summer I had spent in Los Angeles with my aunt. Every day I had climbed her back fence to see the prancing, sleek Dobermans her neighbor was raising. He had a couple of litters of puppies at the same time and I thought they were the most beautiful dogs I had ever seen. Finally, just before I was ready to leave California, I got up the nerve to ask the man if I could have a couple since he had so many.

"Sure," he said with a smile. "Which ones do you want?"

"A black boy and a red girl," I had told him.

"Pick 'em," he said. So I did. Caesar and Cleopatra. Then I had to beg my mom for days before she relented and agreed to ship them back to Colorado with me. As it turned out, the female puppy was stolen out of our yard almost immediately, leaving Caesar a bachelor, so to speak.

Yep, I had picked Caesar out when I was just a boy of fifteen and now I was a man of twenty. I had survived prison life. I had fought to stay alive and kept my manhood. Now it was me and Caesar together again. Two old bachelors!

The rocking of the car as Daddy pulled into the driveway jolted me back to the here-and-now. The car coasted to a stop and we got out and headed for the house. Everyone was waiting for us at the front door.

"Hurry up and get on in here. Dinner's almost ready," Mom yelled from the kitchen. Charmas and my sister Regina stood in the entryway, swinging their arms nervously and smiling broadly. Thurmas signed to me, "Welcome home."

"Hi," I signed back.

I said hello to Thom's wife, Ann, the girl he had married after writing to me for guidance. Ann was a dark pretty girl, very quiet, with big eyes. Tyrone, their three-year-old, was there as well. These were awkward moments. My family was never one for showing outward affection. In fact, Dad and I hadn't even shaken hands at the bus station. And having not spoken for years made conversation excruciating.

After all that time in the Pen, my senses were trained to detect fear. And while that isn't quite what I was picking up now, everyone was strangely cautious of me. I felt like they saw me the way they would a grizzly cub—probably pretty cuddly, but common sense told you to keep your distance.

"Come on now, let's eat," Mom said while herding everyone toward the table. "I worked all day on this turkey and I'm not about to let it get cold. Come on now, Promise Yul, let me fix you a plate."

Everyone seated around the table with a home-cooked meal. This was definitely out of the ordinary for my family. While it seemed slightly contrived, I was grateful for the effort. The uncomfortable silence continued through the meal. No one spoke except to pass this or get more of that, until I saw a roach on the wall.

"Are y'all doing this bad? You have roaches." In Colorado we had played the dozens about roaches. To have roaches there, you had to be poor or nasty or both.

Charmas instantly spoke up. "Aw, man. They don't mean anything. Everybody in Texas has roaches. Even downtown. It bothered me, too, when I first got here, but now I'm used to them."

Once this critical point was cleared up, the deadly silence returned. For long minutes I just minded my plate. So I was surprised when Thomas spoke and said, "Why are you staring at Ann?"

"What?"

"You heard me. Why are you staring at my wife?"

"I'm not staring at Ann, Thom," the surprise I felt seeping into my voice.

"Look, man, I saw you. Don't give me that bull. I saw you staring at my wife," he said scrambling to his feet.

"All right now, Thom, just sit down," I said, also standing. Instead, Thomas came around the table toward me. I could sense how badly he wanted to test me, but he was coming so slowly I could easily have cleaned his clock had I wanted to. As boys we had always teased Thom because he was the shy one in the bunch. The one we all thought was going to grow up to be a fag because he was so quiet. But this time I wasn't going to make the first move. He would have to.

I could hear the others shouting things. Things like, "Stop it! Stop it y'all!"

"Thomas, sit down."

"Promise Yul, don't hurt him."

But it was too late. Thomas moved toward me. I grabbed him and wrestled him to the back door, then let him go. As soon as he was loose he charged me again, like a crazy bull. I was trying not to have to hit him with my fist, so I wrestled. But Thomas had been state wrestling champ two years in a row. It was only brute strength that kept him from putting me in some kind of a hold. Finally, I gathered my breath enough to speak.

"Man, stop! I don't want to fight you. What's wrong with you? I'm not looking at your wife. Don't you remember? I introduced you to her. I knew her before you did, man."

"This ain't right," I heard my mom crying. "Don't you boys know this just ain't right?"

As quick as it had started, it stopped. Thomas straightened up, took Ann by the hand and left. It would be eight years before I was to ever see or speak to Thom again.

Exhaustion flooded my being. The lack of sleep on the trip, the emotion of the day, the stress of trying to reacquaint myself with my family, the fight with Thom, all of it had drained me. Yet in the wee morning hours of that first night at home, I found myself pacing and stirring. Sleep was not a possibility. Every nerve in my body screamed. But for what? For rest? My body wouldn't accept it when I tried. For action? My brain was so spent, it could hardly string two sentences together. For food? I had eaten and eaten well. For sex? The girl in Pueblo had curbed that urge for a while.

The fact was my body was screaming for incarceration. The pressure of being out was almost more than I could bear.

There was no small place I could find that offered me the safety of locked bars. There was no familiar power structure. All the rules had changed. All the faces had changed. All the expectations had changed. I was a jail junkie and I had to kick. But now, I was having the DTs. My body was twitching beyond my control. My muscles ached. I wanted to puke.

As I crashed around the house pacing and pacing I could hear the others awaken. Mom and Daddy whispered in concerned tones. Charmas huffed deeply and sighed often. I spied Regina, just fourteen years old, peeking around the corner of the hallway. Thurmas, of course, slept undisturbed.

I watched as traces of sunlight began creeping in around the corner of the windows. "Oh, God! Please let me sleep."

TWENTY-SIX

"Come on, son. Time to get up now." There was a dull throbbing in my temples. I squinted my eyes tightly against the morning, allowing only the smallest trace of light to penetrate. The sharp pain caused me to close them again instantly. "What you want, Daddy?" I mumbled.

"The man at the gas company said to bring you down to see about a job. We got to leave in about twenty minutes."

My body ached with weariness. I hadn't slept the whole way on the bus to Houston, and I had finally drifted off to sleep about 5:00 in the morning. Now, two hours later, I was *not* ready to face the world. At least not this one.

"You go on without me, Daddy. I'm not ready," I said, purposely leaving the statement vague. I wasn't ready to get up. I wasn't ready to try to deal with the outside world. I wasn't ready to work for the man. I rolled over, turning my back on my dad.

I heard him leave the room and then later talking with Mom in the kitchen. "I'm glad he's out, Fannie, but I don't know if this is going to work or not. He's got to have a job to keep his parole."

"You think I don't know that," Mom said protectively. "Promise, I'm telling you… don't you make that boy leave this house from all your nagging… just let the boy get settled."

Closing my eyes sent waves of warmth across them and eased the sandpaper feeling on the inside of my lids. I slipped back to sleep and didn't regain consciousness for another three hours.

Slowly I eased my way into the kitchen, uncertain if I wanted to run into anyone who might want to talk. I lowered myself into a kitchen chair and, elbows on the table, rested my head in my hands.

The day seemed hot for November. I needed a shower. The more I thought about how long it had been since I'd washed, the more I became aware of my pungent condition. As I stood up, Chum walked in the back door.

"Hey, Prom," was all he said in his quiet manner. I was grateful for his sensitivity to how awkward I felt.

"Where are the towels?"

Noting my ripeness, he didn't ask for clarification, just led me down the hall and pointed to the closet. With no more words passing between us, I closed the door to the bathroom and drowned my uncertainties in a steaming spray of life-giving water. When I emerged, towel around my shoulders, using one end to rub my hair dry, I noticed Charmas was still hanging around.

For the first time since I'd been home, I really looked at the boy. He used to be a skinny little—no, a wiry little kid. Now he'd graduated from high school and had started to work out. He was bulked up. Not only was he wide, but he was thick. And his face had filled out. Somehow he'd turned into a man without me. Aware that these sentimental thoughts jeopardized my mental acuity, I literally shook my head to break free.

"How come you're still hanging around?" My voice sounded gruff, even to me.

"I don't have to go to work for another couple of hours. I got the dinner shift today."

"Where? Where you working?"

"Gallagher's Steak House. Bussing tables."

"Bussing tables? Can't you get a better job than that?"

"Look, it's money. Don't you have to have a job?"

"Yeah, I have to have one."

"Why don't you come with me today? I'll introduce you to John. Maybe he'll give you a job."

"Yeah, maybe. Okay, I'll go. Let me get dressed."

"Oh yeah. About that, Prom." Chum's voice tensed a little, knowing he may be moving out on thin ice. "Let me see if I can hook you up."

Once more I was grateful that Chum had sensed what I needed. Whether his clothes fit me or not, poor fit was better than plain strange. And plain strange is just what the Pen clothing-room clothes were.

I followed Chum back to his room, and as he promised, he hooked me up. Just seeing myself clean and in halfway decent clothes helped me regain the measure of confidence I'd lost since my release.

The day was bright, and as we drove to Gallagher's, I allowed myself the pleasure of chuckling over the farm animals in the neighborhood and a few minutes later ogling the whores on Jensen Drive. The closer we got, though, the more I could feel my underarms dampening under the strain of a pending job interview. I had my DOC certificate with me, but how could I present that to an employer and expect to get a job? The answer is, I couldn't. I took a deep breath. "So, what kind of cat is John?"

"He's the boss."

"I know he's the boss. I asked if he's okay," I demanded. I hated hearing the harshness in my voice. Usually, I could run a situation. But I worried that maybe this situation, being outside, was going to run me.

"I mean, think he'll hire me?" I tried to recover.

Chum glanced my way and shrugged. The rest of the journey we were both silent.

When we got there, Chum introduced me and explained that I had experience as a cook. John and I talked for a while. Since I couldn't give John any good information on where or how I learned to cook, he'd only agree to put me on as a prep worker in the kitchen.

"Take this application home and fill it out. Bring it with you when you come tomorrow and you can work the three-to-eleven shift."

"Thanks," was all I said.

For the third time that day, I had call to feel grateful. Filling out the application at home gave me time to figure it out… not how to put my name in the blank, but what kind of information to put down. How to explain where I'd been and that I had no legitimate job experience whatsoever at age twenty. And finally, how to answer that age-old job application question, *Have you ever been convicted of a felony?*

As I filled out the application, I fantasized about moving up from kitchen prep to Head Chef. It would take some hard work, but I felt up to the challenge.

I liked working at Gallagher's. Tearing up salad, doing miscellaneous jobs for the cook, nothing hard. It gave me time to break in slow. Low pressure. I could do little extras when I wanted to pump it up. Sure, it was boring now, but this was only the start.

There was just one thing about the place that kept me on edge all the time I was there. John never required the knives to be checked out when they were used or counted at the end of each shift, and he also didn't lock them up when we closed down. Anyone could have a knife anywhere, at any time. The situation definitely called for me to be on the offense all the time, so one night I told him, "John, you need to lock up the knives before you forget."

He didn't answer. He just looked at me strange and went into the restaurant. When he came back into the kitchen, I insisted he lock up the knives.

"Go on home," he told me. "I'll take care of it."

The next day I was finishing up around 10:00 p.m., when John asked to see me in the restaurant. Man, I thought, I hadn't even been there a week and I was going to get a promotion and that meant a raise, too!

"Lee, I'm concerned," he began. "You do excellent work around here. Always on time, take pride in your work and I notice you don't mind doing extras... you know, filling the gaps. But back to my concern. About last night. The knives. Do you want to tell me about that?"

"Well, I just don't want to get blamed if one comes up missing," I lied.

"Lee, you ever been in jail?"

There was silence as I studied his face, hoping to find the right answer written there in the lines around his forty-five-year-old eyes. "Why do you ask?'

"Your application says no. What's the truth?"

I was silent, weighing my options, careful not to jump in over my head. "Look, you going to fire me or not?"

"Yes. On the grounds that you lied on your application and I know you've been in prison. I'm going to have to let you go. Pick up your check tomorrow."

I left Gallagher's Steak House, but not for good. I had become acquainted with a white boy who worked with me. He sold dope, mostly marijuana. When I came to pick up my check, he invited me to his house. I went and made some connections and that started my dope selling all over again.

Over the next few months the names and locations changed, but the result was always the same. I worked at a rubber factory for about two weeks, standing on my feet for twelve hours a shift, pushing a button over and over again. If you fell asleep and missed pushing the button, the whole line shut down. The only skill I learned in that job was how to push a button at regular intervals, sleeping with my eyes open, or should I say awake with my eyes closed.

After that I worked at Phillip's Petroleum, filling railroad hopper cars with plastic pellets. I'd pull the lever and wait three hours for the car to fill up. I had a stoke of luck here. I fell taking the trash out and a Spanish guy named Arturo convinced me that if I said I was injured, I'd get a settlement. He was right. I came away with five thousand dollars. Along about this time, Daddy convinced me to join him at the Houston Community College where he was taking courses in refrigeration. "Come on, Promise," he said. "You may as well improve your mind."

I couldn't really argue with him, but I got the feeling that it was equally important for him to feel like he was contributing to my success as it was for me to succeed. So two months after my release, at the start of second semester, I began taking college English, Spanish, sociology, and recreation. There was not much more challenge in college than pushing buttons or filling hoppers, but Daddy was happy and that counted for something.

Anyway, after I got my settlement, I went to work for the gas company as a crewman. What this meant was that I dug ditches all day long, exposing pipes that supposedly had leaks. We didn't use machinery of any type. Just our backs. This time I stayed on for four to five months, until I got just plain sick and tired of digging ditches day after day. Only a little reluctantly I kissed my eight-dollar-an-hour job goodbye.

During this same time, I lied on my application and therefore got accepted to the Firefighters Academy. Now in this there was a challenge. For six months I trained with the other recruits, making top marks in the classroom as well as on the obstacle course and fitness testing. I was set to graduate first in my class. On graduation day, Captain Hollers called me into his office. "Lee," he said. "I've just gotten a letter from Dr. Joyce Gamewell." He paused here for effect. He was a shrewd man. I could feel my lids close slowly as my eyes rolled back in my head. Gamewell had been one of those psychobabble broads who had testified about my psychological condition. She was trying not only to keep me in the Pen but also stated that I should be confined to the state hospital because I would never be a successful member of society. I wondered about the way certain shadows would follow you.

Once again I waited silently for the ax to fall. When I didn't say anything, the captain spoke up. "You know I have to can you for falsifying your application, don't you?"

I didn't speak or nod or in any way acknowledge what the captain said. I just got up and this time, I didn't look back.

Finally, I got a job at the Houston Power and Light Company. I started as a meter reader, and man, I was hot. The meter readers were all assigned to routes and the bottom line was that you had to get your route done by the end of the day. But, if you got it done by 9:00 a.m., you had the rest of the day to yourself, plus you still got paid for the whole day. The other guys took their time, but I always ran my route, had good vision to get a clean read on the meters, and wasn't afraid of dogs. I was soon promoted to Senior Meter Reader, and then, because that was as high as you could go without being a supervisor, I transferred over and became what they called a Field Service Rep.

As an F.S.R., as we were called, I had the responsibility of going out to houses to physically turn the power off or on, investigate if something funny seemed to be going on, and occasionally do some collecting. Man, this was the life. I had my own vehicle with a radio in it, so no matter where I was or what I was doing, I could still get my calls. It freed me up to be anywhere.

Also, it didn't take me long to figure out that this was a powerful position. I could turn on power for anyone, not report it, and just let them pay me directly. I could be the middle man…in the middle between the power company and your bill. It was a great way to make a buck. I felt like I could be set for life, but as things seemed to happen for me, it just wasn't in the stars.

I was backing out of a parking space one day, just minding my own business and legitimately doing my job for the power company, when I heard a thumping in the company truck. When I got out, my stomach sank. An elderly woman was caught in the undercarriage. I must have hit her backing up and then dragged her several hundred feet. She was stone-cold dead. A look of terror was frozen on her face and her hands still clutched her pocketbook to her chest. Shocked, I sat down on the curb, only to find it rise to meet me, jolting my spine.

Eventually, I was absolved of any blame in the hideous accident, but from that day forward, the power company was gunning for me. I had suddenly become a liability. Carefully they planned my demise. They set up a situation calling for my attention as a field rep… a poor woman with a bunch of kids. She needed her power on and I turned it on without routing it through the company. The Sting. The oldest trick in the book. They had me dead to rights. For the third time I sat silent while I got canned.

Always on the side, in addition to the hustling, I'd be doing stuff with dogs. My old Dobe, Caesar, who had been at the fence to greet me when I first got out, was now a well polished, highly trained, and admired companion and guard dog.

One day my running buddy, Frank, said he knew a guy I had to meet. So he took me down to a place called Astro City Kennels. There I got to know a guy named Dan who ran the place. His specialty was Dobes, too, but he also had all kinds of other dogs.

Over a period of months, I started hanging out more and more until I wound up actually working for Dan. He started me cleaning out the pens, then he'd let me work the dogs that were already trained. Eventually, he let me participate in the training sessions. After just a few months, I was bringing in my own clients and training their dogs.

Dan also helped me get started on my own business, a security dog service. I had customers like junkyard owners or mobile home lot managers who would hire me to bring out a dog at night and come and pick it up in the morning. Then all night my dogs would guard their property. Of course, eventually I would explain to them that it would be cheaper if they bought the dog, so I'd make money again.

Sometimes I'd go down to the pound, the boneyard as we called it, and get dogs to train. But mostly, I raised Rottweilers and made money off of them. After I got canned at the power company, the dogs and my hustle helped to carry me over. They were my faithful and familiar paths to making it on the outside.

TWENTY-SEVEN

After two and a half years and a dozen jobs, I determined that I was done working for the man. I had regained my bearings since being out. I had kicked, and I had lived through the withdrawal of being a Pen junky. Now it was time to run the outside like I had learned to run the inside. No more defense. I had to be operating on offense all the way.

All of the jobs I had afforded me the opportunity to sell dope and hustle the ladies. Either I worked days and hustled at night or vice versa. Most of my jobs I kept only for my parole officer, my PO. The three conditions of my parole were employment, therapy, and no more arrests. What they hadn't stipulated was urine analysis. I suppose they figured me to be a hustler and a killer. A hustler is smart enough not to go get high on his own supply. A killer kills 'cause he wants to. He don't need no mind-altering things to take care of business. It comes naturally. In fact, it is the high.

Most of my cousins smoked dope, so I had an automatic market. Since I couldn't work for the man, I decided to *be* the man. And once I had made up my mind, there was no stopping me.

The money I made from hustling carried me over in the times in between jobs. It didn't take me long to figure out when I got ready to move on from a job, all I had to do was wait and quit a day or two after I'd seen my PO. Then it would be another month or more before I saw her again. All during this time I could hustle undisturbed. By the time my next check-in date came around, I'd have another job. It didn't really surprise me that my PO never caught on. She was fresh out of college, young, and afraid. She didn't know whether to supervise or to submit and date me.

When I finally went to work for Houston Power and Light Company and could do my own thing, I started to go with a girl who was the daughter of The *Man* in Houston. He was powerful in all respects and had cocaine for days. So in one move, I became number one son and number two man. Who would have thought that Promise Lee, the Houston Light Man, was also the Candy Man?

I had become so sure of myself in the hustle that I started to let my guard down. I began to get high on my own supply. I was snorting, shooting, and basing coke and a little heroin. Then, feeling a little uneasy with the whole deal, I began smoking PCP. It was a good substitute. Plus, I enjoyed the PCP. It didn't take long to get you high. It was immediate.

I soon got a connection in Oklahoma. Even though somewhere deep down I knew I was struggling with a jones of my own, I continued to work hard at becoming the number one man.

But the coke was, and is, a mysterious thing. Heroin controls you physically, but coke gets hold of your mind as well. I had learned in the Pen and in pimping that if you control the mind, you can control the body. I was out of control because the coke was in control of my mind. I was being pimped by powder. I just couldn't shake it. I got to where I was selling the Wac to support my coke habit. It was crazy.

And the truth is, I was ashamed. Not just that I was out of control, but that I was dealing this deadly poison to people… especially my people… Black people.

It was an endless cycle. Seeking relief from pain, I was doing things that inflicted pain. This applied to all aspects of my life, including women. I sought refuge in their soft, wet warmth and in two years wound up with one, two, three, four kids by three different women. I'm sure this fact in itself caused pain to these women and my children, although at the time, I was oblivious.

Actually, I welcomed the children. Back in my running days in Colorado Springs, I had an accident riding a bicycle on some railroad tracks. The bike tire had slipped off the track and the crossbar had severely wounded me. Blood had soaked the crotch of my bright yellow, bell-bottom pants.

I had been rushed to several different military and civilian hospitals, looking for a doctor who had a clue about how to fix me. I spent about a week in the hospital, but no one had been able to assure me as to whether I would be able to have children or not.

So as pleased as I was to know my capacity in this area, I took advantage of it, regardless of the fallout to my women.

The mother of my two middle children got strung out on cocaine and I got custody of the girls when they were ages two and four. Mom and other relatives really helped out. Even though I was working, I was still an addict with one foot in and one foot out. It's one thing to have custody. It's a whole other thing to be a parent.

This cycle of carelessness and destruction ran its course even in my boxing. It's no news that from boyhood on, it was a priority to me to have good hands. The Pen had given me the opportunity to progress from street brawler to fighter and now on the outside, I had the opportunity to move from fighter to boxer *par excellence*. Through Golden Gloves, I'd had a few bouts in Houston and thereabouts and qualified for the National Championship competition. I could, as the Great One would say, float like a butterfly, sting like a bee. Confidence oozed from my pores and dripped from my lips. I knew I would win!

In 1980, I was twenty-two and living in a house that my Granddad Jeffrey owned with Yolanda, the mother of my third-born, baby son, Mister.

I had a strict training regimen. Every morning I'd get up early, drink a few raw eggs and a little orange juice, and then head out for my roadwork. I was training hard for my Golden Gloves bouts. I had two scheduled for the next day and I was psyching myself up.

Late that afternoon, I noticed that some of the money on my dresser had been moved and that twenty-eight dollars was missing. Yolanda knew she wasn't to touch anything of mine for any reason. It was part of that training... controlling the mind. When I questioned her about it, she lied and said she hadn't had anything to do with it. But no one else could have touched it.

I had to maintain order in my home, so I was relentless in pursuing the whole truth. This time, though, Yolanda wouldn't back down. She stood her ground. The short version of the story is that my boxing dream was not to be. Yolanda and I quarreled throughout the day until I felt I had no choice but to beat her. But then, even after a beating, she wouldn't quit and so the fighting went on until the sun came up.

I used the rising sun as an excuse to fall into my routine. I drank my raw eggs and left for my roadwork. After that I left for the Houston Coliseum, where I had to be early to weigh in.

I was scheduled for two fights that day. The first bout was stopped by the ref in the first round, when I pummeled my opponent.

By the time my second fight came around, the all-night argument began to take its toll. I was exhausted. The ref warned me several times about holding onto the guy, but I was so spent I could hardly stand up, let alone fight. Finally, the ref looked me right in the eyes and said, "Quit holding or I'm going to disqualify you."

I immediately reached out and grabbed onto the guy just to end it. The ref was true to his word and disqualified me.

On the way home, Daddy drove and Yolanda rode in the front seat. Stretched out in the back I was scared to go to sleep. I was so tired, I thought I would die if I closed my eyes.

Once again I had made a bed of drugs and sex and violence and I had to lie in it. It felt bad, but not bad enough for me to change.

TWENTY-EIGHT

N*ow we see in a mirror, dimly, but then face to face. Now I know in part, but then I shall know just as I also am known. (1 Cor 13:8-12, NKJV)*

Even with the disappointment of the Golden Gloves, I knew my money was long and my power was strong. My hustle had given me clothes, cars, women, respect, and even fame.

These things consoled me two years later as I turned my late model Deuce and a Quarter into the parking lot of the 7-Eleven. Everything would be all right.

I jumped out of the car, hopped up on the curb, and headed for the front door. My eye caught the reflection of an image in the window glass. Startled, I felt my heart jump. But the image that had frightened me now intrigued me and drew me near. My eyes were riveted on his form.

What I saw was a dead man. A skeleton covered with paper-thin skin. Its hair was dry and brittle. Its eyes were sunken in its head. It wore a mustache, bristly, and out of control. I moved and the skeleton followed. I stopped and it stopped. My fear transformed into terror. In my soul I knew I was looking at death, waiting to be driven back to hell. I was looking at what was left of me.

I turned around and headed back to my car, confident that what I needed was not sold on the shelves of 7-Eleven. I had already found it in the store's picture window, staring back at me. As I pulled the car onto the street, I wondered how I had changed from a handsome, well-built young man into something that resembled the devil himself. Shame washed over me. I felt naked and alone.

I walked quickly to my apartment and nearly sprinted to the bathroom to look at my face. It was difficult to hold my own eye in the mirror. I sat down heavily on the toilet seat. As I searched for words to pray, I could only recall, "Now I lay me down to sleep." But I didn't want to pray that prayer. I wasn't going to sleep and I didn't want to die. At least not right then. I wanted to wake up. God had spoken to me again and this time I heard him. At least for a while.

I began to cry and soon the words came. "God, help me. Please, God. Help me."

But even as I prayed these simple words, confusion tormented my mind. I had been taught it was wrong to beg God. But I needed help and I needed it right now. So I begged and begged and beg-ged, "God, please help me." My pitiable soul wailed and lamented with a torment that could not be comforted.

After many long minutes, when my head was bursting with the pressure of my tears and when I had vomited forth my aching pleas, I got up off my knees and washed my face and combed my hair. Still feeling the enormous weight of guilt and shame, I showered and changed clothes.

But I felt only a little better.

I went into the kitchen and began throwing away all my para-phernalia. I put it all in a bag, flushed all the dope, and sat my care-fully calibrated dope scale by the front door. It was 2:00 p.m. I got back into my car and headed for the north end of town, for the ken-nel. Just a few days before, I had quit my job there to focus more on my burgeoning enterprise. I went in and told the owner I wanted my job back.

"Fine, no problem," he said. "Go clean out the pens."

There, in the humblest of occupations, I found perfect clarity of thought. There was more joy in shoveling dirt out of dog pens than I now found in the glamour and glitz of a hustler's life.

It was time for this. It was time I came to the end of myself. Drowning, I had to find higher ground.

I recalled sitting on a metal rocking chair in the country when I was eleven and asking my Grandfather Pleze, "Have you ever seen God?"

He sprang up out of his rocker and looking straight ahead like a blind man said, "Come with me, son."

Big Daddy led the way about a quarter of a mile down the road. I trotted along, trying to match his huge, powerful strides. Abruptly, he turned into a cornfield and headed down one of the rows. When we got to a certain spot, tears ran out of his eyes and he began to speak. "Son, I went to church one day and this preacher had a reputation that if he told you the Lord would visit you some morning at six o'clock, the Lord would visit you at six o'clock. So at the service the preacher told me the Lord was going to visit me the next day and so I declare, I was standing right here when I heard the Lord's voice. I heard Him call my name."

The Lord had called my name, too, when I was dozing in the jail cell all those years ago. And he had manifested His power to me today in a convenience store picture window. And even if every man in creation declares it was only the radio back in the jail cell and just the physics of image reflection in the 7-Eleven window, I will always know the very spots I stood when God called my name. And I will remember the very spot in the cornfield where my granddad's revelation began my legacy.

About a year later, my PO transferred my parole to Colorado Springs, where my parents had already moved. I had heard people say that geographical changes didn't matter unless internal changes occur. Deep inside of me I knew I was dying. Even though I thought I was in control of me, I was on a merry-go-round that was making my perception more and more blurred with the turn of each day. I was in a very uncomfortable reactionary mode, like a prehistoric man now living in the twentieth century. I was shaved and groomed to look like mainstream but inside I was in another time frame. I could feel myself desiring positive change but not able to attain it. It reminded me of that old dream, running but going nowhere, just getting smaller and smaller and smaller. I was fed up, the city was too big. I felt like a small fish in the ocean. I needed to get back to something familiar. That's what most people do when they have gotten to the end of their rope. They look for the familiar.

As far as they knew, I had no violations. I had been gone from the Springs for ten years. When I left, I had been building a rep. What would I have to do now to keep it? Promise Lee, lady's man, tough guy, killer, protector, brain, Mr. Courage, pusher, pimp, gangster, and now father.

Everyone had expectations of me. Each person differently. The brothers in the hood expected me to be tough and still in the life. My family expected me to be a rehabilitated model son. My children expected me to parent them. The system may have said they expected me to be a successful citizen in society but really they wanted me to fail, so they could lock me up and throw away the key or kill me.

What role would I play?

Who would I have to be?

It was a blessing and it was a curse.

TWENTY-NINE

In 1983 I had been back in Colorado Springs for two years... in the life. My near-death experience had soon faded in the reality of needing to make a living and needing to make that living in a world that was not interested in forgiving me for my sins.

The questions and doubts I had about coming to the Springs and the expectations of the people here helped to shape my destiny. I had left this town with a rep and folks here made it easy for me to pick up where I had left off.

In a word, I was large. Real large.

In two short years, I had sewn up the dope market in this little town of 240,000. I wasn't pimping in the old sense of the word, but without a doubt I was getting paid.

Yes, I was large and in charge. Nothing was moving in this one-horse town without me knowing about it. I had the power to say live or die. Just that simple. People came to me for favors, protection, loans, advice. A little bit of everything. I was in my element, not afraid to flex my muscle.

It all felt good. It felt like the joint. Even the squares respected me. What else could a convict ask for? What else could any man ask for?

Yes, in a way I had kicked the Pen mentality, but in another, that old feeling of being a convict still lingered. I lived for excitement. It felt good to stick my size tens in a sucker's face once or twice a week. It felt even better to be confronted by the police and be able to dare them to take me to jail.

My life is about having new things to conquer. I bore easily and now there were no more challenges. Once again I found myself searching to fill a void. Searching to quench the boredom.

I began making trips back and forth to Texas and Oklahoma, buying huge quantities of PCP. I began using again. This time PCP.

I suppose it reminded me of the Mad Dog 20/20 in a way. It still didn't take much and didn't take long to mess me up. I found myself smoking it like I smoked cigarettes. It took me out of life and placed me in a dimension that seemed even more vivid and true than my actual reality. But soon even that got old.

I began drinking gin, still trying to kill my boredom and hide my pain. The worst thing about the gin, though, was that it always pushed me into smoking crack. My money was long. I could spend a few thousand every night if I wanted to, and most times I did.

I was returning to the level of those I "served." I was again a consumer, moving further and further away from being a producer. One day when I was smoking crack, I realized that the only difference between me and a crack head was...

Nothing.

But I was a fit crack head. Still priding myself on keeping in shape, I figured I'd find a new place to work out. It was just part of a good offense... never having to use a defense. If I had to get down with a sucker, I didn't want to be there long. One, maybe two, and he should be out.

One thing nice about being in your hometown is that you know a lot of folks, some from the past and some from the present. A few of my old running buddies from times before kept asking me to go to church with them.

They had a spiel. "If you give your life to the Lord, you will have money and a car like mine and wear suits...."

Whenever they started in with that nonsense, I would just look at them. How stupid was that! I had money, clothes, and not a car, but cars. I wondered what kind of God they were serving.

One thing that did impress me about their church was that they had a school and a business, a Fighting Arts Academy.

I asked around to find out where a few of the gyms in the city were and went to check them out. The kind of gyms I liked were few and far between. I didn't want to go to a gym that was known for its appearance. I wanted to find a place where I could be tested and test myself. I decided to try the one run by the church.

One Thursday morning I pulled up in the parking lot, jumped out of my car, and found the door locked. When I glanced down at the open and closed sign, I realized I was thirty minutes early. So I waited.

An hour passed and no one came. I drove to the convenience store to get something to drink, averting my eyes from the window to avoid any ghostly realities and hoping that on my return the gym would be open. It wasn't. I decided to check out the neighborhood, so I made a couple blocks. Still, the sign read closed.

As I began to pull off, a man drove up. He went to unlock the door, nodding, and waving me in. "How you doin'?" he said with a familiar drawl. He sounded a little like me.

"Doin' fine. I just wanted to work out. How much does it cost?"

"There's no cost. Help yourself."

As my eyes scanned the place, I discovered it was not a boxing gym, but a martial arts gym. All the same, I spotted some heavy bags, so I could work out. The man who let me in was named Michael Harp. He had a cool, relaxed, confident, quiet demeanor. He was one I would think twice about physically confronting. As I was taught at a young age, "It's the quiet ones you have to keep your eyes on."

Harp asked me some basic get-to-know-you questions: What is your name, where do you live, etc. He casually asked me where I was from, since my accent was familiar. I told him I had recently moved back here from Houston. Well, what do you know? He was also from Houston. In fact, he was raised not far from Jensen Drive.

As I was getting dressed after my solo workout, Harp asked me where I went to church. I told him nowhere. He invited me to come and visit the place where he worshiped. I had gotten a free workout and he was a nice guy, so I felt there would be no harm in visiting. I told him I would be there, at least for a visit, and I left. I think my non-reluctance was based on his demeanor. There was a certain intrigue about him. I thanked him and headed for the door. I had no idea God had just spoken to me again and that I was finally going to listen.

THIRTY

L ittle did I know that being invited to a church would have such a great impact on the rest of my life. It appeared as if a new chapter was about to begin. To this day, it is still fresh in my mind.

My normal habit of not only being on time for everything, but fifteen to thirty minutes early, was still a large part of me. I sat in the parking lot of the House of Prayer, a small, traditional-looking white church, daydreaming about the satisfied life I was living. There appeared to be no evident void. Everything was going well. I had women. I had money. And I ruled Colorado Springs. It was August 1983—nearly nine years after killing Daniel Hocking. Michael Jackson's *Thriller* was topping the charts and I was thrilled, too. I was only twenty-five and looked forward to a life of more and more of the same. I guess one could say I was finally where I had wanted to be and was on cruise control.

I took a little time to gather my thoughts and make sure my hair and clothing were in order. I wore a tailor-made suit and a medium amount of gold, indicative of a man of power. Then I entered the place that in the past had seemed so routine. My mother and father had sent us to Sunday school every week, but I'd stopped going when I was about thirteen. The only times since had been for funerals.

Two men respectfully and warmly greeted me. This was odd. In the past, all the churches I had attended usually had women at the door to welcome visitors. My eyes scanned the sanctuary as the voice of one of the men politely said, "Feel free to sit wherever you want to."

Why not up front? I thought. *I'll sit right up front, hear the sermon, give an offering, and be on my way.* Most of my life I had sat in the back. Back of classrooms, back of buses, back of police cars. There was no feeling of threat in this place. Why would I need to watch my back in church?

The service began. The music was different from the church music I had heard before. It appeared to have a type of South African/jazz sound to it. The words were different also. The lyrics conveyed current and appropriate meaning. And it was played by a *live band*. Now, that was different. They sang messages of liberation.

We need a liberator.

This is the day of not only our deliverance but also South Africa must be free.

I felt myself being filled with an indescribable feeling. For the first time in my life I felt *larger* than myself. I felt as though I was connected to a greater purpose. This was a high unlike any I had ever felt before. I felt *called*. But called to what? Called to where? For the first time I felt I was a part of something much larger than myself. My mind drifted and I wondered, *Is this how Malcolm X or Rev. Martin Luther King felt?*

The opportunity came for visitors to introduce themselves. I was called to go first and decided to be very brief. I wanted to continue to experience what I was feeling. Somehow I had anticipated there was more to come.

"Hello, good morning."

All of a sudden an uncontrollable feeling of shame swept over me. I was embarrassed to say my name. What I stood for didn't feel positive. On the street, the mention of my name struck high levels of both fear and respect in listener as well as speaker of my name. But not here.

"My name is Promise Lee," I said with what felt like the sound of a small *p*.

"I'm glad to be here. I was invited by the man on the piano."

Then I quickly sat down. Little did I realize the man on the piano was the pastor of the church. As soon as the introductions were finished, he got up from the piano and began to preach. I sat in my seat and felt as though this man I had recently met, who didn't know anything about me, except maybe my reputation, was talking directly to me. The message was as clear as I had ever heard it. It seemed as though all the renegade non-traditional thoughts and ideas I had regarding the purpose of church and Jesus were being summed up and communicated to me right before my eyes. He was the first preacher who understood where I was coming from. He then described a God who was concerned about the systematic injustices of the world—angry at the oppressors and wanting to liberate those who had been victimized by them. He spoke of a Jesus who was not far away, one who could hear my cry, even if it was never outwardly uttered.

He spoke about a God who was looking for people to commission to fight the battles against injustice. He began to describe why this God cared about the oppressive conditions of people because he created us out of love, and people oppressing people was contrary to love–contrary to His nature. He talked about what the Gospel really was—a true story about a loving father who sacrificed his only-begotten son so that all of mankind could be free. Free not only to live with that same Father and Son in eternity, but free to live on this earth as the Father intended. Free from drug addictions, hate, and all manner of sin.

"Hey!" I raised my hand and stood up, interrupting the preacher in the middle of his message.

"I want to know Jesus. I want to be changed. I want to be saved!" The words flew out of my mouth. God had called me again through this man and this time I not only heard, I answered.

I realized I had interrupted the flow of the service, but somehow I also knew that I was in the flow of the service. I proceeded forward without the invitation of anyone and was met by the pastor midway. I felt as though I was under oath, standing in a courtroom. But this time it was a high court, the highest. I gave each of the questions I was asked careful consideration. "Promise Lee, do you believe you are a sinner?" he asked.

"Yes," I replied.

"Are you really ready to give up the life you have been living and exchange it for a new life in Christ?"

I paused to make sure I understood.

"Yes."

"Do you believe in God and believe that God raised Jesus from the dead?"

I quickly said, "Yes."

"Do you believe in the resurrection power of God that raised

Jesus from the physical dead?"

"Yes."

"Do you believe that by that same resurrection power God can raise you from your dead state?"

I said, "Yes."

I have heard the process of salvation described in many different ways, but I can only attest to what happened to me. At that moment I felt as though I had been *born again*. The old Promise had died and there was a cleansed soul and a new spirit in this body.

The service was concluded. Nearly everyone came over to greet me and they seemed to be genuinely happy for my salvation. I couldn't wait to get home. I sang the whole way. When I arrived at my house, I began to take inventory. I wanted to dispose of everything that resembled the me who had just died. And I did: records, clothing, drug paraphernalia, guns, stolen articles, and even my live-in girlfriend. I told her what had happened to me and said I knew this life we were living was wrong.

"You have got to go." And she did.

All this happened that same day.

As evening drew near, I called my mother and told her what had happened. There was a moment of complete silence and then came the tears. This time they were tears of joy, not pain. She began to tell me how happy she was and how proud of me she was, but the thing that I remember the most is her saying, "I have been praying for you a long, long time. The good Lord has answered my prayers."

Now I just wanted to be alone to think about all of this. I felt free because now I was free. Normally, this time of night I would be out on the street hustling. Tonight I was at home not even answering the phone. Then I realized I hadn't had a drink or a hit of dope all day. The realization wasn't prompted by desire but by simple recognition. Where was the appetite, the craving? It was gone. Could this be true? Could God do all of this in a matter of moments? I had used drugs for most of my life and now the desire was gone. I sat right there in my chair and felt His embrace.

THIRTY-ONE

The first days and weeks after that were different. A week later, I even gave away my car. I had been fighting pit bulls for money and got rid of all of them as well.

There was a slowing down.

There was less rushing.

There was a calm and a peace.

And at the same time, I was lost. I felt a void, somewhat like the space between exhaling and inhaling. I had exhaled the old life but hadn't quite inhaled the new. I had moved instantly into a whole new world and new style of living, and I didn't yet know the rules. Born again, I was indeed like a baby. So many internal and intangible things had just changed inside of me—emotionally, mentally, intellectually, and spiritually. It was as though I was in a different supernatural culture with a different economy and I wasn't sure my ATM card would work. Or if I even needed one.

I was like someone coming into the realization that they had been bound and now were free, but not knowing what to do with the freedom because of being bound so many years. I felt empowered, and yet so many things were different. It was like when I was freed from prison and didn't know that phone calls were now twenty cents. So it took me back to those days. I had learned how to be free and had even succeeded in that free world, at least in terms of my old way of thinking. I could do it again in this infinitely freer world I had just entered.

This forced me to look introspectively, which is often uncomfortable. For the first time, I could clearly see the damage I had done to myself in my ignorance and came to a realization of how childlike, immature, non-caring, and insensitive all of my actions had been. I felt grief, thinking about the people I had hurt: my family, Daniel Hocking's family, the families of the men I'd murdered. The women on my "list." The children I had sired. The live-in girlfriend I'd thrown out on the street. I felt a similar naiveté in this new state of grace. Would I in some way regress and become what I was in prison? Would I unknowingly hurt even more people before I found my footing on this new shore?

Gradually, I came to realize that there were many practical lessons and good habits I could transition from my prison experience into my new life. I had spent years defining and refining some of the skills that helped me survive and even thrive while incarcerated. I didn't need to throw it all away. Like a quilt, I could take that piece from the past and patch it with this piece from the present. I thought about the character I had developed in prison. By character I mean the very essence of who we are, especially when nobody's watching. My character was based on how I would react under certain pressured situations and circumstances. I had developed personal strength and character while I was locked up, but it was layered with a lot of foolishness. I began to sort the wheat from the chaff, groping for my character's good parts.

One of the most important things I'd learned in prison was to keep my word. If you didn't, whether it was about being somewhere at a certain time, or that you were going to kill someone, everyone would know they couldn't count on you. You couldn't bluff.

I also learned to fast in prison and did it a lot, sometimes intentionally, sometimes not. I had stopped eating pork the year before I was arrested, so if all they gave me was a bologna sandwich, like when I first arrived or when we were in lockdown, I didn't eat. My studies of various religions, like Hari Krishna, Baha'i, and Islam, revealed that fasting was a spiritual practice. As I tried out this form of discipline, I realized why, as my sixth sense and all my other senses became keener. I was able to tap into another realm, to see the unseen and hear the unspoken. I came to "know" that something would happen, or have the potential to happen, before it did. This gave me an added advantage and helped me to survive.

I had learned to contemplate while being in jail for many of the same reasons and with many of the same benefits. Now I returned to this practice and began to spend a lot more quiet time. It didn't mean everything around me stopped, but everything did change. I had always gotten up early and most of my life, on autopilot, jumping out of bed and into my day-to-day dope transactions. Now there was a lot more time for meditation, soul searching, and looking deeper into myself.

In prison, I had learned that the strong survive and vowed to never be on defense again. If a person can't abstain from a meal or from cigarettes or drugs, you are not in control but actually out of control because things are controlling you. I learned through experience that fasting doesn't move God closer to us; it moves us closer to God. Martial arts also showed me how to develop my offense while helping me to learn self-defense techniques and to center myself. I was tapping into yet another level of power. I decided to keep up my physical training and to give up cigarettes, though this last decision and its fulfillment were some months apart.

I had also learned that family was important. In prison you need friends to watch your back. Now I began to spend more time with the men who were part of the church, joining in for various fellowships. This was a way to watch my *spiritual* back. To sustain my new life, I needed new playthings and new playmates. I also began to spend more time visiting my parents. They lived across the street from Prospect Lake, which had been one of my main dope territories. Before, I would be across the street from their house, doing deals. Now I was sitting on the porch having family discussions.

I learned to write letters in prison. I had written them for Old Petee and I had written them home. I had written them to girlfriends and I had written them to Tom Armour. I vowed when I got out that I would never get too busy to write a letter. Some of that had stopped over the years. I went back to writing to my grandparents, other relatives, and to my friends who were still behind the prison walls.

In prison I learned to value nature because we got to see so little. The sky or the stars or a tree would be so rare. Since getting out, I could see them day in and day out, if I would look, but my mind was usually on other, dead things. Now, in the new realm I was experiencing, I could not only see a tree but know what it was communicating to me. It was like that brief moment in the prison yard when I saw the stars and knew my dreams were calling me to where I was now.

As I began to fashion my new self, it was almost like trying on a new suit. Suits nearly always need alterations but the fact of the matter is that you're not a tailor, so you're dependent on someone else to do it. My new birth inside happened in an instant, but I lived in the physical world and faith, without works, is dead. I needed to choose the practical, everyday actions that would define me as a man who had turned his life over to God. And it wouldn't all happen that same day or same week. It was a process. And only God knew how it would unfold. Only God.

THIRTY-TWO

Most people didn't seem to know what to think of me. Even though I had become a Christian, in the minds of many there was doubt. Some people thought I was just running a game. I suppose it was too early to tell whether or not the new Promise was real. My mother believed in me, but the rest of the family was skeptical and unsure, especially my siblings. Thom still kept some distance. Regina had grown up only hearing and knowing the bad things about me, so she was slow to believe I could be different. Charmas, who had always wanted to be like me, got into trouble *after* I dedicated my life to God.

My friends thought this was a fad or a phase or another con.

But they would all understand in time.

I had tapped into a new source of power.

It appeared that everything I desired to do or have was being granted to me. I had been used to paying cash for everything. Now with poor credit, I needed a vehicle. I went to several car lots and was turned down. But when I saw the vehicle I wanted, I laid my hands on it and later that day it was mine.

I would visit people in the hospital, lay hands on them, and they would recover. In fact, my faith in God was so strong, regardless of the weather report, I would pray for certain types of weather and God would grant it. As I look back, I think it was because God wanted to reveal His power to me and largely because I was in the will of God and asking and seeking things that were in line with God's heart. I had finally aligned my heart with His.

Yes, it was true. God had performed a miracle in the life of Promise Lee. I was a new person. I continued to grow in Christ by carefully examining my Bible and attending church. The street life was over for me. Somehow God had taken away my appetite for the things that bound me for so long. Drugs, women, temper, violence, killing—everything that had kept me away from God were now permanently removed from my life.

Except cigarettes. Six months after my conversion and I was still smoking. I never saw myself as an addict, despite the overwhelming evidence that all the men in my dad's family had two strong addictions—coffee and women. I never drank coffee because I didn't want it to have control over me. Somehow, I hadn't applied that same thinking to women. Prison helped me break the woman thing, as I developed personal discipline. My addiction was not so much to sex as it was to manipulate and control. I guess I was an addict after all.

People turn to addictions because of appetite, to medicate, to numb pain, to deny. I think people can become even too addicted to their religious practice and that can prevent them from really *experiencing* God. Dogma can cloud our vision so that we fail to see the truth, thus preventing us from experiencing and moving into the benefits of the realties. I always wanted to be in a place where I could learn and entertain new thoughts and ideas, but my vision was still clouded by cigarettes.

After all the changes I'd made, couldn't I hold on to this one habit? Part of me thought it was okay to still be a smoker, but if it was okay, why was I concealing it from everyone? I began to question this new life in Christ. God was powerful enough to remove the appetite for the hard stuff, even my long-ago established addiction to women, but He couldn't take away the cigarette habit? I was confused. Finally, I realized it was not God who was holding onto the habit. It was me. I foolishly thought that *I* could quit anytime. Here was God speaking to me again, but not in what had become the familiar audible voice. This time He was speaking to me through my foolish pride. God wanted me to realize that there are things I could not do on my own, even if I had made the decision. *Change occurs in more than just a decision.* That day I prayed and prayed and prayed for God to remove this crutch. But during and after all that praying I felt no relief. Here I was, being controlled by three and a quarter inches of paper and tobacco.

I took my pack of Kools and put them in the trash can. Then I closed myself up in the closet. I told God I wasn't coming out until He took the desire away. I prayed and cried out to God as though it was a matter of life and death. It was. Some three hours later I emerged from that closet with victory. The cigarette habit was gone.

Around the same time I heard the voice of God again, not audibly but on the inside and through a dream, telling me to preach. *God, this is the last thing I want to do.* I didn't want to be up in front of people, especially because my past early images of preachers were a huge turn off. Nevertheless, I answered the call. One Sunday morning I told Pastor Harp about my visitations from God.

He confirmed it.

"Promise, God is calling you to preach."

"Preach? When and where would I do that?"-

"Whenever God gives you a word to preach, just let me know."

So it was. It happened a few weeks later. One Saturday night I just couldn't get to sleep. I tossed and turned for hours. Finally, I got up to read my Bible. I randomly opened it to 1 Samuel 17:4. It was the story of David and Goliath. I began to read and write.

The next thing I knew, it was daybreak. Time to get ready for church. I arrived before anyone. When the pastor pulled up, I told him the Lord had given me a word. He looked at me with reservation and finally said, "Okay, you can preach this morning."

When it came time for preaching, Pastor Harp got up and announced that I would be delivering the message that morning. I had about thirty pages of notes and had written in my Bible so much that it was unreadable in places. I came up from the pew, stood behind the pulpit, and proceeded to read my notes.

Somewhere out of nowhere a wind came in and blew most of my papers off the podium onto the floor. It was impossible to gather them all up and it would have taken forever to put them in order. So I tried to read from the remaining ones. Strangely, my eyes became blurred and I could not see what I had written clearly.

God, did you really call me to preach, or had I misinterpreted the dreams and other signs? I found myself frozen, standing there silently in front of two hundred people. Then I opened my mouth to say I'm sorry, but those are not the words that came out. God had laced my mouth with the words he wanted the people to hear. I had studied, written notes, prayed, and meditated on the scripture, but as with the cigarettes, it was on Him that I needed to depend for the power to accomplish the task at hand. The sermon went well, especially for a first timer. From that point on, I learned to do all I knew to do and allow God to breathe on it. I have given many hundreds of sermons since.

THIRTY-THREE

Since I was no longer going to earn money in the ways I did before, I had to get a job. I went to the school district and applied. On job applications it asked if I had been convicted of a felony since the age of sixteen, and I always said no. I had been convicted the month before I turned sixteen. Some people in the district knew about my past and refused to hire me, even though my answering "no" to the question was technically true. Just because I'd been born into a whole new world didn't mean it would be easy.

I threatened to sue, so they gave me a job.

I started as a paraprofessional helping Phil Johnson, the gym teacher at Sabin Jr. High, which was a predominantly white school that was just beginning to attract other ethnicities. Phil knew about my record and advocated for me. I enjoyed a connectedness with the students because I wasn't viewed as an authority figure, but as someone who really cared. I used my knowledge of people to turn their energy into positive things. It wasn't the first time in my life that I felt like a role model, but this time it was for the good.

All this time I was an active member of the House of Prayer. When you're multitalented and can multitask, you get to do a little of everything. I was quickly placed over the building maintenance, sweeping porches, and shoveling snow. On Sundays, I arrived first to open and was the last to leave. In the early eighties, as a reaction to the anti-apartheid movement in South Africa, Black churches across America were being torched. Some local churches, including ours, were spray painted with Nazi swastikas. I painted over the swastikas and spent some nights in the church, protecting it. I also got to travel with the pastor as his assistant when he spoke in various cities.

During this time, I made a job change when I got an offer to come to West Junior High School as the track coach and community liaison. I was the only Black working at the school, which was predominantly Latino and white. I stayed there for a few years, during which I designed a track field and park behind the school and successfully lobbied the city to pay for it. I also coached the girls' basketball team and took them to the finals twice, once winning second place in the city. This had never happened before in the history of the school. I did the same with the track team. Our team of twenty kids took second out of all the district schools, most of which had fifty to a hundred kids.

I also started several alternative programs for kids. When someone wouldn't show up at school, I'd go looking for them. At that time there were a number of satanic cults in that part of town. One day I went to an area called the Ruins to check on some kids and found them involved with this. With some help from the police department and, of course, the Lord, I broke up this ring.

A few years later I got an offer from the Care Coalition, a nonprofit established by a dentist and others to combat substance abuse. My job was to run a federally-funded program for young Black boys ages ten to fourteen who lived in single female-headed households. I developed life skills programs and rites of passage for these young men that incorporated Black history, camping, intellectual survival, boxing, and martial arts. I was fortunate to travel around the country to speak at universities and other forums about this premiere program and became part of the national lecture circuit of the governor's program to reduce or eliminate illiteracy, drugs, and unemployment. God was preparing me, adding skills I would need in order to serve in ever-widening circles of his work.

THIRTY-FOUR

I grew up in an area of Colorado Springs that was called the South Side, then Lower Shooks Run, then Hillside. It was a close-knit community of one thousand homes, predominantly Black, with a few white single female head of households—often the German wives of soldiers. There were also some Mexican residents, who mostly lived on the perimeter. Hillside had older houses with front porches and was family and community oriented.

Everyone knew everyone *and* their business. If John was beating his wife or Lois was an alcoholic, you knew. Some corner stores, like a fish market I remember, were family owned. When you walked in, they called you by your first name and you could get stuff on credit. All the kids went to Helen Hunt Elementary School and South Junior High. My friends and I went to the Boys' Club after school and in the summer, and we could swim all day at Prospect Lake for a dime. In this sheltered world, we were poor but didn't know it. The world outside our community was something else. At that time in Monument Valley Park, they would drain the pool after Blacks swam in it. But Hillside was our safe haven.

When I returned to Colorado Springs, Hillside was a whole different world, with drugs, prostitution, and gangs. The city had neglected the area, and only the crooked police would come there. The entire sense of community had disappeared, replaced by predators, not only on the street but in downtown offices, in terms of lending and redlining. South Junior had been the community center. South had been *ours*. It was the only school that was primarily Black and Mexican, and even today, many of its athletic records still stand.

When attempts to integrate the school, by bussing in white students failed, the school district closed it around '79, when I'd been away for about five years. This devastated the community and the neighborhood immediately took a turn for the worse.

One Sunday, a few months after my first visit, a strange thing happened at church. I came up to the altar in response to an invitation to receive prayer. The pastor's wife laid hands on me and began to prophesy. She said I was called to be a man of great influence, a political leader, that I would do great things in this city and around the world. I went home that day, not really understanding what all that meant. I had no desire to be great and certainly no desire to become a political leader; I didn't know anything about politics.

That evening, four senior women came to my home and said, "This neighborhood is in terrible shape. Dope houses everywhere, prostitution, gangs, and other crime. Promise, you messed it up and it's up to you to fix it."

Wow! What boldness these women had. Of course, that came as no surprise. These were some of the many women who had seen me grow up in my neighborhood. And, as I thought about it, they were right. I was the one who messed it up and it was only right for me to try to fix it. They asked me to put the creed into the deed. Faith by itself, if it is not accompanied by action, is dead (James 2:17) and I wanted my faith to live.

To galvanize a group, you must either reveal a crisis or create a crisis. After those senior ladies had come to my house, I hand typed a newsletter with statistics on area crime and called for Hillside neighbors to band together at an organizational meeting. The ladies helped me hand out the newsletter to every home in Hillside and they also helped to spread the word through a telephone tree. I rented the Helen Hunt gym for our first meeting and told God that if we had at least twenty people, I would know this was something I should pursue. Sixty showed up. After a series of meetings, we founded the Hillside Neighborhood Association and I became its first president.

Hillside had been neglected for decades, so our first goal was to upgrade the neighborhood. Every time we would deal with one issue, it would shed light on another part of the neglect. Crime was prevalent because there were hardly any working street lights in the neighborhood. Alleys had excessive trees where people could hide out. We got the city to trim the trees and pave the pothole-filled dirt alleys, so they would be utilized more by the common people.

We also asked the city to upgrade the parks. The playground equipment on the south side of Prospect Lake was the same I'd played on twenty years earlier. On the east side of the lake, all the equipment was new. Two hundred Hillside neighbors showed up for the meeting that city representatives attended and made their desires known in no uncertain terms. The various upgrades began slowly and were completed in less than a year.

Next, we turned our attention to the drug problem. I had established dope houses, I knew the game. I had information and had always been told information was power. But this was going to be different. This understanding of rooting out evil was going to take faith. Information is power, but faith is assurance. My past reputation remained fresh on the minds of wrongdoers and this worked in my favor. I went to every dope house in the neighborhood and politely told them to close shop. In some cases, I explained to them the damage they were causing to the kids and other people in the neighborhood.

I would typically walk up during the daytime. Sometimes there would be a guy standing guard at the door. Everyone either feared or respected me, so they let me in. I'd knock on the door and the point man inside would open it. He oversaw the living room, where people would be sitting and waiting to do business. He'd usher me through another room, where people were purchasing the stuff, and then to the back part of the house, where some people stayed to smoke. The air would be filled with clouds of crack smoke. That's where the main man was. I'd go back, pull him to the side, and talk to him. There was always another extra room for the head guy, and we'd usually talk in there. I remember one guy telling everyone else to leave because he knew what I was coming for. He called his security guys in and I talked to them all at once.

"You are killing this neighborhood with this dope. Not only is it negatively affecting the adults, but the kids also. You've gotta shut it down, man."

It didn't surprise me that most of them closed up immediately. However, "There were some kings who didn't know Joseph" (Exodus 1:8). I had to use different approaches to get them to close shop. I somewhat shamefully admit I threatened them. Sometimes there would be some dialog and debate.

"Well, if you're not going to," I'd tell them, "I'll take it to the next level."

"What? Are you going to snitch? Get the police involved?"

"No. It's something I can do all by myself."

That would usually be enough. At that time, the Black Muslims had a program called Dope Busters that was federally funded for a while. Sometimes I took a few Muslim brothers with me. They always wore bowties and suits, but if they had to use force, they would. And the other brothers knew that. I'd like to think the dope houses closed down more from respect than fear. They'd just move it to the next neighborhood, but at least our neighborhood was changing because we were changing the community norms. When you do that, the old norms are no longer acceptable.

After we closed down the crack houses, we tackled the issue of quality affordable housing, turning our attention first on the slumlords. Certain homes in the neighborhood had been poorly maintained and not really fit to live in for a long time. We began putting pressure on their owners in two ways. One was word of mouth. We'd just let the neighborhood people know this is not a good place to live. When prospective renters arrived, neighbors would warn them, "Oh, you don't want to live there. Let me tell you about this landlord...." We also put pressure on the city code enforcement department, reporting code violations that were not being enforced. The city would send a letter and it would be so expensive for the landlord to fix all those long overdue things, they would be receptive when we started negotiations about selling the home.

We partnered with local banks to help residents get affordable loans and become homeowners. We also partnered with Habitat for Humanity and a Denver organization that worked with Fannie Mae. When I-25 was being expanded, I saw in the newspaper that several old Victorian houses by the highway were going to be demolished. In Texas I had always seen houses lifted off the foundation and moved, but that was a relatively unknown practice here. Our association collaborated with the city of Colorado Springs and the housing authority to move them onto a two-acre spot in Hillside Heights.

Next, we took the city to task regarding the unequal distribution of resources, such as for federal monies and other funds. In 1995, we created a No Tolerance program for drugs, illiteracy, runaways, and crime. Residents who agreed to the No Tolerance campaign used yellow porch lights and yellow ribbons to indicate safe houses where kids could knock on the door and seek refuge. This sent a clear message out to the negative elements. The program won national attention and was emulated by other cities.

After being run by volunteers for nearly ten years, we wrote grants to the governor's office for community organization efforts and also received some money from local foundations, so the association could become self-supporting. We began to initiate a membership fee of one dollar a year per person, which over time increased to five, then ten dollars, with twenty dollars for a family. We were renting the space for our offices and one day found out the owners were going to sell the whole plaza, so we launched a capital campaign to buy it. The asking price of the building was $150,000. We raised $50,000 in six weeks, mostly from the neighborhood. People brought in bags of pennies and coins that had been hidden in their houses and old bills folded up that had been under their mattresses. We also had a few large donors. With enough for the down payment, a friend at Wells Fargo Bank did some creative lending, and we were in!

In 1997, we were blessed to win the National Civic League's All America City Award. This is the oldest and most prestigious community problem-solving award in the country, bestowed for the highest level of civic excellence. This was the first time in the history of the award that a neighborhood was the recipient. It is usually given to regional, state, and local governments. Vice President Al Gore personally honored me for this work.

I felt privileged to have been a part of all this and in a sense, I felt redeemed because I had made amends for the damage I'd done to my part of the city.

THIRTY-FIVE

D uring this period of my life, I learned the difference between career and calling. In the first year after my conversion, I was provided the opportunity to give sermons two or three times at the House of Prayer. With each one, I felt far less nervous, more confident, and more validated in my calling as a communicator. Still, I wasn't so comfortable with the thought of being called to ministry. Most of my evangelism had been one-on-one or in the parks and neighborhoods I'd previously destroyed. Pastor Harp was such a great communicator, no one would have felt confident in his shadow.

When he left that church, I was asked to head things up because of my gifts in administration and my connections in the community, but I didn't feel capable or qualified. I stayed a couple of months and then heard God speaking to me and telling me to leave. For a while I was out there, wandering, practicing my faith, but without a home for that faith.

I had been celibate since I gave my life to God. It wasn't hard. I did exclusive dating—I guess they call that serial monogamy today—but I wasn't sexual. I directed all my passion into cleaning up our community. I was so consumed with Hillside work, one female acquaintance complained that she'd be walking around with short tee shirts on and I hadn't even noticed her. That just wasn't my focus.

I had been raising my two daughters alone and decided I needed a female role model for them. About two years after my conversion, when I was twenty-seven, I decided to look for a wife. I was introduced to a young woman who grew up in church. Her father was a Pentecostal minister, and she sang in the church every week. I thought, *We can be a team to win souls for Christ.* We had four children in our years together. Our life was the church. After a while, things began to flounder and I realized we needed an identity of our own. One day I said, "We've got to leave this church. Are you married to me or married to this church?

"I am not leaving my dad's church," she answered.

During the divorce I got custody of our children and three of them came to live with me, so I was now the single parent of five. I realized that I had been looking for a nanny, but instead I needed to be looking for a wife. A little over a year later, I met and married Juanita, a wonderful, sensitive, mature and beautiful woman, who takes my breath away.

We initially established Relevant Word Ministries to come alongside existing poor churches and help them in board development, youth programming, and grant writing. I traveled around the country doing this for two years, but the poor congregations couldn't support this ministry, so it folded. I supported my family with a grant to do community organizing and I was still on loan to the governor's office as well.

I always felt that when God moves people toward change, the million dollar question is, what church do you send them to? People kept urging me to start one. That was the *last* thing I wanted to do. I'd seen what happens in much of the Black religious community. The sacred office of minister has so often been abused and poorly represented. If someone was not successful in life, they would simply hang a shingle out and say God had called them to preach. And yet, most of the significant Black leaders like Martin Luther King Jr., Louis Farrakhan, and Malcolm X have come from the church. God kept speaking to me through the voices of other people and finally I heard God's call to start a church ministry in November 1997.

Actually, what I decided was to try and fleece God. *All right. I'll do it. We won't advertise, it will just be by word of mouth. If you send ten or twenty folks, I'll know for sure it's you and that you have called me to this.*

We rented the Helen Hunt Elementary School gymnasium for one Sunday, set up chairs, and sixty people showed up. How ironic. We were in the same hall where we had organized the Hillside Neighborhood Association, I'd set the same goal of twenty people, and the same number of people showed up. I guess God wanted to make sure I got the message.

Nevertheless, the next week I upped the ante.

God, if folks will give their lives to you, then I'll know for sure it's you and that you have called me to this.

The next week during the service, a wino who was walking down the street stepped into the gym, stood at the back, and heard the word.

And finally, so did I.

Many years have passed since then. Sometimes I think about that little boy so long ago, watching the bees die. Death has been a constant companion to me, but so has the chance to be born again. Every day I die to the old as I live into the next wondrous chapter of God's plan.

Well, more than twenty years after my conversion, my story goes on and on. At the time of this writing I am not dead. Tired, but not dead. And definitely not bored! After holding Sunday services for a year or so at the elementary school gymnasium, attendance had grown enough that we moved our services into the local community center for the next six years. In August 2004, we moved into our permanent building—an even larger platform from which to bring a message of empowerment, compassion, and hope to this multicultural community.

We now offer a variety of empowerment programs including: job training and entrepreneur development, economic development, youth leadership training, intergenerational programs and a host of other opportunities. We have also started a multimedia recording label. Juanita and I devote our lives to one another, to our eleven children, and to spreading God's word. My mission has expanded into a broader advocacy for justice for the poor and disenfranchised, including the incarcerated, the homeless, the addicted, and the oppressed.

Along the way, I earned an Associate degree from Pikes Peak Community College in Social Work and Bachelor's and Master's Degrees in Christian Counseling. I am currently enrolled at Fuller Theological Seminary working toward a doctorate. I am considered an activist and speak internationally on topics of leadership, male empowerment, and at-risk youth.

My desire is to expand the already established ministry in Honduras and to help the economic development of the Miskito (an obscure and forgotten indigenous group of Hondurans), living in the remote village of Wisplini, and to empower them to live prosperous and productive lives through the practical application of God's Word.

As of this publishing, I have petitioned to have my records

sealed, however, the District Attorney's Office has denied my request. And although I have already received a pardon from the Highest authority, the Creator, I am in the process of requesting a pardon from the Governor's Office of Colorado and am hopeful it will be granted. I plan to write more about my *new life*, which has had and continues to have its struggles. If you think my life as a child growing up in the streets without God was interesting, wait until you hear how things have been on *this* part of the journey, as an adult with God at the center of all I do. I have had encounters with angels and demons, and I have experienced innumerable miracles. I stay in touch with those still incarcerated and encourage them to hold on until their change comes.

Life has taught me how fragile the so-called human spirit is. It can be damaged or broken very easily. I have offended God because I have damaged the souls of his children, and it is the soul of mankind that God is most concerned about. Over the years I have hurt many people, both intentionally and unintentionally.

Each day I ask God to help me to do less harm.

Wake up wake up man
take that dope out yo hand

Can't you see
it's a trick of the enemy

Come on baby girl
get your mind on the real
world

It's easy to figure
you want to make your pock-
ets bigger

No way can you become a
millionaire
sitting at home drawing
welfare

And you baby boy
that crack ain't no toy

It has two objectives
to kill and destroy

Instead be strong, throw that
pipe away

It's mind over matter
life or death which would you
rather

I hear you saying in your
mind, I'd stop if I could
If you knew what I knew, no
doubt you would

As I've said before you got to
be strong
Please my people leave that
pipe alone

You say you want to quit, well
that's a good sign
But it takes more than words
lounging in your mind

You'll always be tempted time
and time again
Remember this fact, that pipe
is your enemy not your friend

Ask God for will power,
strength and grace
that's the only way out from
this crippling place

You have a chance, you ain't
dumb

Stretch your hand to the master, He's the one

Time continues to move on
while you think about back
when

Saturate yourself with the
Word it will prove to become
your friend

Because it's only on God's
word that we can truly
depend

And just remember, when in
doubt, don't move a pawn
Stand still, be silent, adhere to
the voice of the Great One.

Promise Lee, 1980

Reverend Promise Lee currently resides in Colorado with his wife Juanita and family of eleven children and four grandchildren. A nationally-known and sought-after speaker, Reverend Lee is Senior Pastor of a rapidly growing multi-ethnic ministry that teaches empowerment through the practical application of God's Word. He not only uses his experience and God-given talent to share messages of hope, but to also invest in America's most precious commodity—people. Because of his unique and versatile style of information delivery and bridge-building, he has spoken to a diverse population in a variety of settings including colleges, universities, businesses, seminaries, churches, ministries and special interest groups. His message of personal responsibility and independent empowerment has helped elevate the thinking of individuals and groups.

For information and scheduling, please contact:

RELEVANT WORD CULTURAL CENTER COLORADO SPRINGS
1040 South Institute PO Box 17592
Colorado Springs, CO 80935

(719) 635-6640
relevantword.org